Snowbird Gravy
and Dishpan Pie

Patsy Moore Ginns

J. L. Osborne, Jr., Artist

University of North Carolina Press

Chapel Hill

Snowbird Gravy and Dishpan Pie

Mountain People Recall

© 1982 The University of North Carolina Press

Manufactured in the United States of America

Library of Congress Cataloging in Publication Data
Main entry under title:
Snowbird gravy and dishpan pie.

    1. North Carolina—Social life and customs—
Addresses, essays, lectures. 2. Mountain life—
North Carolina—Addresses, essays, lectures.
3. North Carolina—Biography—Addresses, essays,
lectures. 4. Oral history—Addresses, essays,
lectures. I. Ginns, Patsy Moore. II. Osborne,
J. L. (Jesse Lee), 1923–
F259.S66   975.6   81-16296
ISBN 0-8078-1516-0   AACR2

Dedicated
with love
to the memory of my father,
Hermie Dudley Moore,
whose stories would have been
very much at home within
the pages of this book

Contents

Chapter Three. Child Life 42

Chapter Four. Of Work 63

Chapter Eight. The Community 144

Chapter Nine. Mountain Stories 172

Chapter Ten. Ghosts, Haints, and Witches 184

Preface

My father was one of those hardy, independent souls of Scotch-Irish stock who peopled the slopes of northwestern North Carolina. Many were the times he would undertake a task solely with grit and persistence.

Throughout my childhood and far into the years of my middle life, I lived to the tune of the anvil's ring. My father would, perhaps, be hay-making when the mowing machine would break down, and while the mules stood and waited, he would take to his homemade smithery out in the edge of the woods by the stable, where he would persist until he had the particular piece of metal mended—or had fashioned a new piece entirely. He might have turned the mules out to pasture and spent a good two days at the job, but when he finished, back on the old mower it went, and the haying would be done!

This fiercely independent pride in the work of one's hands was only one of the marks of stamina that undergirded the soul and character of our forebears. Courage and determination accepted the challenge, and despite whatever obstacles presented themselves, the task was surmounted. In the words of my father, "You just went ahead and did whatever had to be done."

However, when the week's work was done, nothing pleased my dad more than to sit by a neighbor's fireside and reminisce. Picture, if you will, two or three seasoned old "gents," as he called them, reared back in straight chairs as they chuckled their way through an evening's yarn swapping.

This, too, was an inherent part of their culture. Each had his favorite turns of phrase, and although the experiences recalled were at times stark and grim—as life in the western half of our state often was—it was always recalled with a bit of whimsy, a good-hearted humor that blessed it all. As Dad would say, "I remember when all we had to eat was po'k and grits. You'd just po'k your feet under the table and grit your teeth!"

And so, like the ring of the anvil, the mellow richness of my father's voice as he began a tale of "an old fellow that used to live over here . . ." is one of the lovely, lost sounds of my childhood.

Whether it be the experiencing or the sharing of life such as this, many of us feel that we are no longer in touch with this element of our culture, and we continually hunger for it. Thus, the purpose of this collection.

In this, my second volume of oral history, the words of a retiring generation are recorded verbatim. This time, the voices speak from the western Carolina mountains, those historically rich and sometimes remote areas which lie between the gently rolling Piedmont and the boundary of Tennessee.

Again I have traveled, tape recorder in hand, to visit with people on front porches, around the family woodstove, at Senior Citizens' meetings and food service programs, and out in the berry patch to collect accounts of life as they remember it. These are seldom the prominent or the celebrated; they are, however, the everyday people who have helped to transform the fully timbered wilds of our land into the familiar countryside which we all know. These are our grandparents, neighbors, and friends. Their voices are our second nature. Their words fall into "found poetry" the way raindrops drum out their melodies on a tin roof.

Also, once again, J. L. Osborne, Jr., has added his drawings to illustrate the character of a people and a land. A North Carolinian himself, he has a special gift for bringing memories to life with pen and ink.

The material here has been organized by subject, and the remembrances span the approximate time from the 1880s to the Depression era. The name of the narrator, year of his birth, and county are recorded at the end of each selection.

This continuing work is a collaboration between narrators, publisher, artist, and collector to preserve personal accounts of life in North Carolina from a period of time fast fading into history.

Direction and assistance have come from a number of people, but especially from librarians and library workers who operate bookmobiles throughout the western North Carolina mountains.

With gratitude and endearment, we present the following collection.

Snowbird Gravy
and Dishpan Pie

Chapter 1. Of Mountains

The western North Carolina highlands are both beloved and deeply respected by their people. Though the rugged terrain often proved resistant to settlement and winters were habitually forbidding, the tenacious settlers held on, entrenching themselves on the ridges and in the valleys. With determination of soul and sweat of honest toil, they have molded their lives around these slopes.

Home Again

I was raised over on Buffalo Creek,
Little Buffalo,
they call it,
under the Bluff Mountains.
We could just sit out in the yard
and look up at the Bluff
anytime.
I've been up there
many's the times.
It was beautiful!
It's still beautiful!
I like the mountains.
I've been out a few times,
down to the lowlands,
but I was always glad
to see the old mountains
a-loomin' up in the distance.
Glad to be home again!

Hazel Campbell, 1893 Ashe County

A Trade

Our folks come from England. My great-grandpa first settled in Wilkes County, and then he settled up here in Watauga County.

He entered two hundred and sixty acres of land for twenty-five cents an acre.

Later, he couldn't feed his family; couldn't clean up enough ground to feed his family with that. He settled up here in 1770-some; we found the record at Boone. And he traded his land off for a black-and-tan dog, a sheep hide, and a hog rifle — a muzzle-loader, a Kentucky muzzle-loader. You load it in the end with black powder. Then later on, he came up on another piece of land and traded it.

See, he could take this dog and this rifle and kill game and feed his family, but he couldn't clean up enough ground to raise enough to feed 'em.

Now, the sheepskin, he had it to sit on, or if it rained, he could put that over him to keep from gettin' wet. Maybe wrap it around him when it was cold.

And I said, my great-grandpa let me down the drain. Give the land away, you know.

See back in them days there wasn't no roads in here. There wasn't nothing. Now, my grandpa walked from back over here in Spice Creek in Watauga County, walked from there to Madison County, to his folks. He married out there, and he'd take his old hog rifle and walk through the mountains. Take his stuff along with him to eat, kill stuff along the way, you know. Said it took him two weeks. 'Course you can drive it now in about three hours.

He just followed the ridges and found his way through it. And then he took him a hatchet and blazed it so he could go back.

Just by hisself. That was a hard trip for him to make. Now, when me and my wife was first married, we walked to Boone and back.

Stanley Hicks, 1911 Watauga County

Linville Falls

Another thing my grandfather told me
about Linville Falls.
Where the falls pours off now,
it's worn down through the rocks.
And he said
in his time
he saw it pour over the top.
The last time he was down there,
I walked down there with him,
and he said,
"Can you believe
it has worn down that far?"

Winnie Biggerstaff, 1904 McDowell County

Murphy

Oh,
Murphy was beautiful back then!
I had a friend who used to say
that if she didn't live in Murphy,
she'd move here!

But we didn't have any paved streets,
and when it rained,
the mud would be at least a foot deep.
But the city got huge boulders
and put them here
to use to cross the streets.
And that's the only way
you could cross the street
in rainy weather.
Oh,
the mules and wagons,
they just got in a rut.

People were spread out all through this region.
They lived up in the mountains,
and they lived on huge farms.
The ones that are living right in town now,
some of the families are still living
in the same houses
that their parents built.
I've never lived in any other house.

Emily Cooper Davidson, 1894 Cherokee County

Our House

When I built my house and covered it in boards, it blowed snow in the house, and me and my wife would have to put the quilt over our faces to keep the snow off. Then, get up that morning and walk through the snow in the house where it blowed in and feed our chickens through the cracks in the floor. See, they'd go under the house, and I'd feed 'em through the cracks in the floor.

Now, people will think, "He's just telling that," but that's the God's truth! Ain't no joke; that's a fact!

You'd just live or die, son. That's just the way it was. No, not hardly any of us died then [from exposure]. You see, then people walked about everywheres they went to work. Had nothing to ride. You walked there, and you walked back.

Well, now they'll get in a car or get in a truck and ride to the job. Then they'll ride back to the house and set and watch television. Then they drop over from heart attacks and die. Ain't a-gettin' no exercise. That's the reason of so many heart attacks now, just as sure as we're a-livin'.

We never heard nothing about no heart attacks then. People didn't have no heart attacks. Most people died of old age then, just get real old. I mean, they lived to be old. My wife's grandma was a hundred-and-some years old when she died. And then, my first cousin was a hundred-and-five. Now they get about forty, fifty, sixty, and they drop out.

Stanley Hicks, 1911 Watauga County

Back to the Mountains

Most of 'em come back.
They go away
in their younger days,
but then,
when they get older,
most of 'em
want to come back to the mountains.

Ralph Crouse, 1922 Alleghany County

Chapter 2. Home and Family Life

In the Carolina mountains, home was a haven against the elements —most of the time. In the early days, it was not unknown for Mother to climb the ladder into the loft and sweep up the snow that had sifted through the cracks during the night before she could light a fire below. Else, it would "rain" on the breakfast table.

From oats grown and cradled by hand would come the morning hoe-cakes, and when times were especially hard, bread-crust coffee filled in for the real thing. Thrift was not an empty platitude but in many cases the necessary means to real survival.

Yet, life within the home was rich and warm. There was no question about one's belonging to a family so close knit and interdependent.

Setting up Housekeeping

When we was married now,
well, we was married in 1932 or '33.
I couldn't tell you which.
And what we had to start out with
was a feather bed and a feather pillow
that Mother gave me.
One pillow.
Her mother give her two quilts
and one pillow and a sheet.
And we went and bought us a bedstead
and give six dollars for it
at the second-hand store.

Dad give me a bushel of corn.
And her mother and daddy
give her a hog ham
and a poke of flour.
And Mother give me one old pan,
two forks,

and one spoon.
Her mother give her
two or three little dishes,
maybe cracked or something.

And we went to a sawmill shack.
Rented a shack where they had sawmilled at.
Stayed there two years.
Worked on the farm for people
for a bushel of potatoes a day
and a piece of meat a day.

And, in later years,
we got to where we could clean up
a new ground
and raise us some stuff.
Me and her would go out
and clean up new ground.

And she washed,
went to people and washed
and cleaned up houses
and done work like that
for twenty-five cents a day.
And I cradled oats and worked on farms
for fifty cents a day.

We picked up chestnuts
in the fall of the year
to buy shoes and clothes with.
And we'd carry them about ten miles
to the store.
Buy our stuff,
put it on our backs
and pack it home.

I'd buy overalls like I'm wearing now
for thirty-nine and forty-nine cents a pair.
Now they're fifteen dollars.
But I can get the fifteen dollars now
easier than I could get the forty cents then.
Much easier.

We raised our hogs,
had our cow and got our milk and butter,
and our chickens and got our eggs
and raised our stuff to eat.
We eat what we raised
and raised what we eat.

And my grandpa
made the first pair of shoes I wore.
He was a shoemaker.
I was about nine
when he made my first pair of shoes.
What'd I wear before then?
Well, near about nothing,
just to tell you the truth.
Went barefooted near about all the time.

Now, when I got grown,
after I was grown at home,
we got one pair of shoes a year.
One pair a year.
And them was drove full of tacks,
and we'd go to the shop
and have heel irons made.
Put 'em on
so the heels wouldn't wear out.
Brogans is what we'd buy.
And we'd buy 'em about a size or two big
so they'd last.

We'd get just one pair of shoes a year,
and before we'd get our shoes
in the fall of the year,
we'd go to run the cows up every morning.
You know, the frost was on the ground,
so we'd run 'em up
and where they'd been laying,
we'd go stand in their places
to get our feet warm.

Stanley Hicks, 1911 Watauga County

The Depression

I was born in 1922, and the Depression struck in 1929. And boy, she was rough in this mountain! That made it bad. There was no work to get no money, to get no clothes with. People could have made it good, a-raisin' a little crop for food; but where they had it at, was they like to have froze to death with no clothes, shoes, no money. You had plenty to eat if you worked and raised it, but [nothing for] your clothes and a little extra, like if you wanted coffee.

Now, Mother made bread-crust coffee. Now, the crumbs of the bread, she rationed it. Us kids, we just got to eat what she put in each one's plate. And it was light!

We kept a hog, and she fried the meat, the what-they-call pork; we called it "hog" all the time. Anymore, they call it "pork." She fried up what she cut every morning off that meat, and nary one got to run in like children do and grab and eat up from the other one. She divided it and put what you had to eat in each one's plate — for dinner, supper, and breakfast. I's so thin the wind would blow me down. Weak, crying, seein' death every day. You couldn't lose no money because you didn't have any.

But Hoover hoped it there. He paid it out, had it nearly out of debt. But boys, people punished! It was awful how little kids — and some didn't look ahead — now, if the parents would look ahead and raise the food for the children, they wasn't that many punished.

And a lot of banks went busted. A lot went crazy, took their lives because of it. One feller that married my mother's sister lived down yonder under the hill, had his money in the Butler bank. It went busted, went bankrupt, and he had seven hundred dollars, he said, in it. Seven hundred dollars, you know, back then meant something. You was called a rich man with seven hundred dollars.

And so he'd go to the woods to stay, and them a-talkin' to him, his wife and children, finally brought him back. He made it, got brought back. And it built back, then. He finally got three or four hundred of it back. That was from the next bank that started back in Butler, Tennessee, back there.

He was the only one, at that time, in this country that had enough money to put in the bank. And he'd just eat his crop, what he growed. He worked and saved every penny. He was one that said that he never thought of dimes, that he thought of saving pennies, and pennies made dollars. And he saved up seven hundred dollars in about thirty years there, twenty to thirty years.

Made his own shoes out of his cowhide. He made his own shoes and turned the hair on the inside, and boy, they was warm! Made him a last and pegged 'em together. Made his, his wife's, and all of the children's shoes. That's the reason he saved up that little money, where the others didn't. Had plenty of shoes to wear.

Made his steer harness and his horse harness. He bought nothing except a little salt and sugar.

They's a lot of 'em, back then.
I can remember Grandmother, down here,
and my grandfather.
Now, they'd buy a little brown sugar.
Hardly ever buy any white.
Sweeten their berries a little with it.
And it was put up in the cupboard.
They really trained the young'uns
to leave it alone.
It was for company,
when they come.
And a lot of 'em would want to save it
to show to their neighbors, too,
if they was a-comin'.
Feed 'em good,
and then they'd have to starve for three meals after they left.
Make 'em believe,
and after they left, they'd say,
"Boys, Mr. Hicks is a-comin' out of it!"
See, they had sugar for dinner or for breakfast.

Ray Hicks, 1922 Watauga County

A Sledrunner House

When I was growing up, we were building a new house, and my father had all this material ready, and it was on the bank of Cranberry Creek, down across the South Fork of New River. He also had a store. General store.

And the flood came. Now, this happened about 1916. Well, the flood came and washed the store away. And it washed all the new building materials away. I can barely remember the flood, but I remember crying and saying I'd never have any more new dresses.

And sometime after that, he bought this boundary of timber up here and decided he'd go into the timber business. He bought it from his father and his mother.

It was down on the old soapstone quarry.

There were three of us children. And we had this house, something like twenty feet long, on sledrunners. Yes! On sledrunners!

And in it we had an old cooking stove. On the wall there was a table that fastened with hinges, and in the floor were the places nailed on where the legs of the table went. So when we got ready to eat, my mother had to raise that table top up and put two legs under it, put the chairs around. And then we'd eat, and when we got the dishes all washed, we'd let the table down.

And in the other end was a bed that was nailed into the wall, and we'd let it down and put the mattress, feather bed, or what-have-you on it. My father and mother slept on it, and maybe the least child.

Then about ten or fifteen feet from the door we had this tent. It was quite large; it had three or four beds in it. I remember it had a dresser. Of course, we didn't take everything. And we had planks on the floor to walk to different places. So we stayed in there during the summer — and also during the winter.

Had to carry water from a neighbor's home. And we stayed there that winter. Then that next spring, as the work went farther toward Bald Mountain, we moved a little closer to it. So we took the sledrunner house with us. And when we went to move that house, my father just put two oxen to it.

Lorene Dickson, 1908 Ashe County

The Springbox

We used to keep the milk and the butter in the springbox. Everybody had a spring, near about. And they had a little trough coming down through the springhouse. The water would run in a little trough.

And you'd put your butter and milk down in there to keep it cool. And if you had a well, you could tie a rope on it and let it down in the well to keep it cool. Let it down twenty, thirty, forty feet to get it down where it would stay cool.

But in the spring, see, this spring water was usually around fifty-five degrees, and it'll keep milk and butter for several days at that temperature.

Ralph Crouse, 1922 Alleghany County

Cherokee Indian Life

I have lived here all my life. Life has changed a great deal. It was a whole lot different when I was growing up.

We lived in a house like the one I have over there. When I was growing up, it wasn't as cold then as it is now. We cooked outside on an open fire. The fire was built outside even in winter.

People didn't seem to mind the cold here. We went barefoot even in winter; didn't have shoes. There was no fire in the house, just outside. We didn't notice the cold. I just wore a dress, and just run out in snow barefooted. We didn't catch colds, flu, or pneumonia. Mothers kept babies on their backs most of the time.

Children didn't have any toys, just playing in mountains in daytime, climbing around on trees. Nowadays, we would be scared to let children do that. People made toys from corn stalks, pine needles.

No wild animals came to the house. Nothing ever bothered us. Mother used to grind meal for our breakfast. I went fishing with grandmother to have the fish to cook. In the summer, we would eat greens and berries for our meals.

We ate bear meat. Built a big fire and put meat over it, then hung it up. We would cut meat up in little chunks and put them on sourwood to give flavor, then hang it up inside the house on the porch. Nowadays, if you hung up meat for a day, it would spoil. We used salt on meat when we hung it up. Did rabbit meat the same way. We would smoke and salt it. We wouldn't eat it now, but it was good back then when I was a little girl. Dried all the food for winter and lived on this. Our people ate two meals a day back then. Now, I eat three meals. Snacks, too.

The bear lived somewhere in a log, and Indians would know where and go look for it. Used sharp sticks to kill bear. Used bow and arrow; they went in pretty deep through the skin. It would kill bear any size. Deer, also. We had tame hogs. They just roamed all over. Didn't put them in pens. Let them hunt their own food. There were a lot of chestnuts for them to eat. We didn't brand our pigs.

Men would go hunting. That's all men had to do. All women did mostly was grind meal.

When we washed clothes, we did it in a peculiar way. We made our own soap. Hollow out a piece or part of a tree and put clothes in there and beat them with a board or paddle. The clothes would come clean, though.

Some made their own cloth from sheep wool. There were no clothes around here to buy. Some got cloth from across mountains in Tennessee. They would buy it and make their own clothes. Also used animal skin.

We didn't have all these things we have now. Houses were made out of logs with holes for windows. Chimneys out of rock. Regular doors out of logs cut out. People made their own nails out of wood. Made their own hinges too. The wood just fit into the place for the door.

I would carry my baby on my back, and when got tired, the father would carry the baby. When we were walking long way, we would stop and rest. Put the baby down and let it play around. We carried her until she was three years old.

To punish children, we would use a real small stick and switch on legs. Our daughter has grown into a fine girl.

Way back, men and women didn't get married. It just came about later. Two people just got together and stayed together for life, didn't separate. They didn't get into arguments to separate them. Both man and woman were the head of household. Both agreed on things.

Maggie Wachacha, 1892 Graham County

Note: Maggie Wachacha is a Cherokee Indian lady held in high esteem by the Cherokee Nation. She speaks no English, only Cherokee. The above interview was conducted by means of an interpreter.

A Mother's Life

My grandmother, Mary Fairchild, was the mother of nine children, five girls and four boys. And she said that my grandfather, Thomas Fairchild, would be away on a carpenter's job, and she would be there with the children in the summer. And there would be the crops to make, but there would also be the cooking to do for the children.

And she said, "I would have plenty of fresh vegetables in the garden, but how do you work all day in the field and have something cooked for the next day?"

So she said, "When we would get all the work done, and we would have our supper, then I would take a lantern and go down to the garden and pick beans, and I would gather whatever I needed to gather to cook.

"Then I would go to the house, and I would get all of this ready. And," she said, "next morning, I would get up in time to put all this in the pot and cook, and as soon as it was light enough, I would get the children up and we would go out to the barn and do the work. But all the time, my food was cooking. Then, as soon as we had breakfast, we were all ready to go to the field again."

And yet Grandmother Fairchild lived to be in her nineties.

Marie McNeil Hendrix, 1913 Wilkes County

Making Apple Butter

During the Depression, you had no money to amount to anything, and you couldn't get sugar. And you couldn't get much flour.

I remember my mother cooked apples. We had lots of apples, sweet apples. And in cooking apples, she used apple cider to sweeten them. Cook it down.

And she always saved a cupful of sugar.
Somebody might get sick,
so we always had a cupful of sugar.
But it was hard to get.
When they were sick,
we'd use it to sweeten tea
or something of that kind.

She made apple butter with the cider and molasses. I remember we had a great big pot that they used to make the apple butter with. And they had a cane mill to make the syrup. They used lots of spices. Made it like you would apple sauce. Kept stirring. Did it outside. Used a big old washpot.

They boiled clothes in that pot and then they'd clean that pot and make apple butter in it. Used syrup and spice.

Now, this cane they used for molasses is not regular sugar cane. It's molasses cane. And they had a press that it ran through that was turned by horses. They caught the juice and put it in the evaporator and boiled it down till it made syrup.

Kate Hayes, 1892 Cherokee County

Applepeel Pie

Apples was scarce one year. Real scarce. My grandmother had a half bushel of apples. She canned the apples, and then she taken the peelings and canned those. Washed 'em real clean and canned 'em.

My mother said, at the time, "I'll never eat those." But then later on, she was down in the hayfield, and when she came in, my grandmother had baked two wonderful pies from those peelings. And my mother ate three pieces.

They used so many things that we throw away. I remember Grandmother peeled the potatoes real deep and planted the peelings. Raised our potatoes that way!

Winnie Biggerstaff, 1904 McDowell County

Snowbird Gravy

And, you know, back when we growed up, years ago, just kids and all, we'd catch snowbirds. You know what snowbirds is. And we'd clean 'em up, put 'em in the pot, and make gravy out of 'em. Oh yeah! Makes as nice a pot of gravy as you've ever seen if you get enough of 'em.

So we'd take a barn door. You know, just take a door off of a barn, put a trigger under it, and put a string to it. Just hide it in the barn.

Then we'd just put all kinds of oats and stuff under there, and when fifteen or twenty got under it, we'd jerk the string. Then we'd go get 'em and have enough to make a pot of gravy.

So there was an old man stayed right close to us. His wife was about blind. Couldn't see. And he was a-gettin' some too, you know. He caught a couple. Just got two and said to her, "Now, you make some gravy for me out of these for breakfast."

Well, had these old pothooks, you know, across the bar that you'd hang the pots on. And then you'd put 'em in there in hot water, boil 'em, and make your gravy and all.

So she couldn't see, and she went in to put the birds in the pot. And she pitched 'em over behind the backstick. And so she worked and kept a-boiling this water, and the birds over there behind the backstick.

And, I don't know, me and Dad went down there for something that morning. We'd done got breakfast. Went down there a little late, and they was a-eatin' breakfast.

And the old man, he was a-dippin' in there, and he said, "Mary, this snowbird gravy is awful weak. It's terrible weak. I just don't believe there's no snowbirds in it."

She said, "Yeah, I put 'em in it."

He said, "I just don't believe there is any in it. Honey, I just can't find any. Mary, I don't believe they're in it."

She said, "I throwed 'em in it last night."

He went back and looked, and they was in behind the backstick, back in there. That got him. He was eatin' his gravy off of snowbirds, and there wasn't any snowbirds in it.

Well, now, you have a backlog. That's to throw the heat out of the fireplace. Then you put your other fire here, you see, and she had throwed 'em behind that backlog. See, it's a green one, bigger than the rest of 'em. About a ten- or twelve-inch one.

A snowbird, I'd say it'd be about an inch and a half through. There wasn't much to it, just the breast, but it was good. What it was was real good.

Then we'd take a stick and put in 'em. We'd kill 'em, we'd go out and kill 'em and dress 'em and then take and put a stick in 'em and take and hold 'em before the fireplace and put salt on 'em and broil 'em. Pull 'em off and eat 'em.

You just about had to survive on what you could get, you know. I can go out in the woods right now. I can take my rifle and my little old 'seng hoe that I dig herbs and stuff with and put me in the woods, and I can — no bread nor nothing — and I can live all through the summer without ever comin' in to the store for a bite of anything.

Take me a fish hook; stuff like that. See, if you come to a groundhog hole or a ground squirrel that's went in the hole, you know you can't get it out.

Just go get you a bucket. Get you some water and just start pouring water in the hole. Pour the water till the hole comes full and starts runnin' out, and get you a club and stand there.

It's a-comin' out. You know it's a-comin' out. So just knock 'im in the head, dress 'im out, and there you go!

And if you come to a rabbit hole, and it won't come out, just go to pouring water in the hole.

There's many ways to survive without just going out here and gettin' it easy. I've done a many a one that way. Just stand there with my stick, and when it pokes its head out, bust it! Get him for my meat, you know.

Us boys, we'd go out and camp that way, maybe, for two weeks. Just for the fun of it. Kill groundhogs and eat 'em; kill rabbits and eat 'em. Stuff like that.

Now, a groundhog, all that greasy part you cut out and throw away. Just get the parts you want. Get them kernels out under the four legs. You've got kernels there that big [measures], and if you cook 'em, ain't nary dog can eat one. It'll stink and run you out of the house. Cut all them out. Cut these ribs off; throw 'em away. Get all the fat off.

Cook it about two hours, two to three hours. Then pour all this water off and put it in a pan after you get to the house, and put it in the stove. Bake it. Just strip them big pieces off!

'Coon is the best meat I ever eat. That's better than groundhog.

Dad used to, we used to 'possum hunt a lot. You could sell the hides for twenty-five cents apiece. Polecats [skunks], they'd bring about two and a half. We'd trap 'em, catch 'em. That's the way we'd have to do to get a little bit of change.

So Dad would 'possum hunt, bring 'em in. And he'd say, "Boys, let me have that one to fatten up." So he'd feed 'em milk and bread for about two or three weeks. And then kill 'em. And you talkin' about something to eat, son, they was good! They was tender and good; they was better than chicken.

And the funniest thing happened! We was standin' on the river over here. You know, bullfrog hams is good to eat. You can survive off of just about anything like that through the summer.

So Dad went down to the river, and I went down there. And there was a big old bullfrog down there. I caught it, and it was a awful big one. Took it up there to him, and its hams was that long [measures]. He just took a stick of stovewood and knocked it in the head.

Now, to catch him, I had just slipped up behind him and grabbed him. He was in the mud partly, you know.

He kept a-bellowin'. You know, he'd go like a cow bellowin' or something. This was about dark. So he took it to the house and knocked it in the head. Then cut its hams off. Legs. Dressed 'em out and took 'em in the house.

And then the next day, Mother was fixin' 'em for him for breakfast. We didn't have nothin' much to do that day, and the sun was gettin' up. It was gettin' up in the morning, I'd say about seven o'clock.

When we didn't have anything to do, we didn't get up too early. When we did, we'd get up at four o'clock.

So Dad, he was sittin' there eatin' these bullfrog hams, you know. Said, "Boy, them is good." Well, the window was right at the table where you could look right out to where he had throwed the old bullfrog.

Well, that old bullfrog was out there. He hadn't killed him, you know. That thing was sittin' there with his mouth goin' open and all. He'd just knocked him in the head.

I said, "Dad, look a-yonder."

Mother said, "Oh, Lord, you're eatin' that frog's hams! Go out there and do something with him."

And he said, "The dad-burned thing! I'll get it after awhile."

Stanley Hicks, 1911 Watauga County

Jerk Coffee

One old man,
now, he was so stingy —
this ain't no joke; it's a fact —
he took coffee beans,
and he dried 'em in the stove
just about like you'd fix a peanut.
Then he took a string
and put a hole through several beans
of the coffee,

put the string through it.
Wouldn't let his wife bother it.
Called it "jerk coffee."
Then, he'd hold the coffeepot lid up
and hold these beans down in here
on this string
and let it stay so long.
Then he'd jerk it out.
Hang it up,
let it dry,
and use it again.
And that's what's called "jerk coffee."
I'd call it water.

It ain't no joke. I'm a-tellin' you the truth! Then they got to where they'd save the grounds. They'd buy 'em, make their coffee, and then they'd take 'em out and put 'em on a board and let 'em dry. Then they'd go back and make it again. Which it got very weak toward the last of it.

And that's the way the thing went, just to tell you the truth. There was a lot of stuff then that people don't fool with now.

Stanley Hicks, 1911 Watauga County

Sweet Hickory Salet

My grandpa said he took these here sweet hickories—I don't know if you know what they are or not—but took the leaves off of them early in the spring to make salet out of 'em. Sweet hickory. Get the leaves off of 'em just like you'd go and get salet out of your garden. Yeah, they were grown trees. Eat 'em.

Now, there was tough hickory, and there was sweet hickory. You can dig the roots out of it, and the roots taste sweet. But there don't many grow around this country.

And they'd dig out artichoke. You know, now they've got that tame. But he said then they'd dig them out and eat 'em when he was young. They was wild.

Stanley Hicks, 1911 Watauga County

Hard to Get a Nickel

We'd take our wheat to the roller mill.
Raise our wheat and take it to the roller mill
and have it ground.
And we eat that.
And we growed our cane and made our 'lasses.
And Mother would take and ball it up
and make coffee out of it.
Just keep a-cookin' it and stirrin' it
until it just got to be in a ball.
Then she'd make coffee out of it.
Ground it up in a coffee mill.
See,
it would be hard, like candy.
It tasted pretty good.

Then we parched corn
and made coffee out of it.
Parched wheat
and made coffee out of it.
Parched chestnuts.

And take cornstalks,
the pith out of 'em, now,
you know the pith in cornstalks?
She'd burn it to make soda with
to put in the bread.
Just burn it into ashes
and then put it in your bread.
Put it in a pan and put it in the stove
and burn it.
Then she crumbled it up
and put it in bread
and made soda out of it.
And that would make the bread rise.

If you bought soda,
you could get it for a nickel a pack,
but it was hard to get a nickel.

Stanley Hicks, 1911 Watauga County

Using Lye

Experience is the best thing a-making hominy. Well, I make it with ashes and drip that lye. I use the lye, you know.

Have a bucket with holes in the bottom and put a little straw in so the ashes won't go through. Hang it up first; then you'll pour the water and it'll run through, just as clear.

Then you have your corn. Well, heat your water to hot, and don't pour too much of that lye in at one time. It'll eat it up, maybe. Sometimes it's stronger. I've never heard of anyone getting sick off of the lye. Some use Devil's Lye, but that'll eat you up.

When it goes to boiling, if you don't think it's going to be enough, you put more of that lye in. Then you take a spoon and lift up some grains and see if that husk is a-going to come off it. Just mash it with your finger. Now, don't use too large a-grains; the little grains skins better and cooks easier.

And then you wash that husk off good, and you put it back and cook it until it gets done. Why, it takes hours to cook it. I made some last winter.

Nannie Smith, 1888 Clay County

Dishpan Pie

You know, we didn't have no cans to can nothing in. We dried our blackberries. And in the winter, we'd take those dried blackberries and make 'em into a pie, just the same as if they were fresh. Put 'em in a pan, put some water in and let 'em go to boiling; then put your bread in, your dough. And that was good!

And peaches.
Peaches was the finest things dried,
you know.
People enjoyed eating then
more than they do now.
Oh, my goodness,
I guess they did!
They worked harder,
and they enjoyed their food more.
I'd bake dried apple pies, tarts, fried apple pies. In some things, I

believe the big old iron pots give the food—some of it, anyway—a
better flavor. Now, where they boiled cabbage—you know, put a big
bone of meat in and boil cabbage—now, that was really good! We had
cornbread with it.

And soup beans! I used to have half-a-bushel of soup beans. Those
were the white beans you grow, and the hulls were tough, and you
shelled 'em. People would make great big old potfuls of stews, soups.

And when I had my children at home, you know, I'd make a pie in a
dishpan. One of the smaller dishpans, you see. Crust on the bottom and
a crust on the top. Now, that I baked in the oven, after we had an oven.

Iowa Patterson, 1881 Clay County

A Bachelor's Life

Now, I do all my own canning.
Hot water bath.
Don't pressure cook 'em.
Too hot, too fast!
And it'll kill 'em.
Ain't no use nobody arguing with me
that it don't!

Canned fifty-five half gallons
of them beans last year.
Didn't get much corn.
Coons got my corn last year.
I can anything anybody else does.
When I've got it,
that's what I can.
Can turnips.

Ain't but one thing I season.
When I open a can of beans,
I put my meat in with my beans.
If you ain't got it,
and you can't buy it,
you don't do it!

I used to hunt squirrel, rabbit;

'possum hunt, coon hunt, and all that.
Them days is all gone.
You can't hunt nothing up here
but a dang deer and a coon!
Don't care a thing about deer.
You could bring one up here,
dress it out,
and I wouldn't take it in the house
if you give it to me!
That's the nearest nothing
I ever tried to eat;
and turkey is the next!

Now,
chicken,
you can go out here and buy.
Has the flavor of chicken.
Now,
I got one of 'em the other day
that tasted like chicken.
When I got it fixed right,
it tasted like chicken we used to have.
I make dumplin's with 'em,
if you know what that is.
That's the way I fix 'em.

Ain't nothing hard to do
if you just don't look at it like that.
Can't get no cornmeal no more.
Ain't nowhere you can get it ground.
You buy it,
and it ain't meal;
it's flour!
They don't know where to stop a-makin' meal
out of it.
They make flour!
I make buckwheat bread, altogether.

Ain't never been married.
Gettin' along fine by myself.
Oh, yeah!
Ain't never been to the doctor

but one time in my life.
Constipated.
That was the only thing
that was the matter with me.
Course,
I had the mumps, measles, right here.
Got over 'em.
I was a boy.

Drunk sweet milk one time.
Got sick.
Quit right there!
Don't drink it no more.
I do not.
I drink buttermilk
if I know who makes it.
I'm just a little bit queer
about my eatin'.

Don't have nobody to complain to but myself.
I don't complain much,
and nobody who ever eat here
ever complained.

I've just always been a hard worker.
Don't worry about a thing.
Never did!
Nothin' ever worries me.
What use is it to worry?
What good does it do?
If it's gonna happen,
let it go!

Tom Pruitt, 1904 Alleghany County

Five Hundred Fruit Jars

And if we didn't have two hogs
that would dress five hundred pounds apiece,
why,
we didn't have no meat.
My daddy would say,
"We ain't got no meat.
What are we gonna do?"

It wasn't like it is this day and time.
You have hogs dresses to about
a hundred and fifty
or two hundred pounds.
But back then
they wanted them dressed
five hundred pounds.
Salt-cured it
and canned a lot of meat.
And then,
if you killed a beef,
why,
that was usually all canned up.
Well,
there was six of us boys in my family,
and if you didn't have five hundred
half-a-gallon fruit jars full,
you didn't have nothing much to eat.

Take a half-a-gallon of cherries
or blackberries,
it didn't go far
with six boys eating out of it.

Ralph Crouse, 1922 Alleghany County

Sousemeat and Livermush

Now, when they killed the hogs, they used all the parts of the hog—all of them. Out of the head they made head-souse, which was cooked, and you'd put vinegar over it and let it set for several days.

Just ground the head meat up and put pepper and salt and vinegar in it. Course, they took the bones out and cooked it real tender before they mashed or ground it up. I can remember my mother-in-law mashing it with her hands. They didn't have a grinder at the time.

And they made sausage from the scraps. And, of course, they cured the shoulders and the hams and the side meat. Back then it was cured with white salt. We didn't know what this Morton's salt was at the time.

Then after about four or five days, we'd go back and salt the bones again, around the edges of the bones. And after twelve or fifteen days, then, you could hang the meat up. Finest thing in the world, I guess.

We made livermush from the liver. You know, we buy it in the store now, and it isn't fitten to eat. Always, when I made it, I cooked the onions and everything with it—salt, pepper, and onions. And then we'd make it out in cakes so we could slice it. It sure tasted different from what we get now.

Winnie Biggerstaff, 1904 McDowell County

The Lesson

And these students, they come up here and wanted to kill a hog, you see. And so I told 'em to go buy it.

So there was seven of 'em. Seven of 'em went in and bought a shoat; I guess it weighed about, I'd say, a hundred and fifty pounds. Dressed out about a hundred. And they brought it over here. Ha!

So I built up the fire and got the water and everything hot. And I said, "Well, there it is."

They said, "Who's a-gonna shoot it?"

I said, "There's the rifle."

"No, you shoot it. We'll make it squeal."

I said, "Well, I've made 'em squeal, too."

They said, "You shoot it."

So I shot it.

They said, "What do we do now?"

I said, "You stick it."

They said, "Stick it with what?"

I said, "Cut its throat. It's a-gonna die, so cut its throat so it'll bleed."

They said, "You do that."

So I took my knife and cut its throat. And then scalded it. And I've got a bell scraper, so I told 'em to go ahead and scrape it.

They said, "We don't know how."

And I said, "Well, you won't learn no younger."

And they messed with that hog. Finally at last, I just got tickled so good I just couldn't live. I'd have to turn my back or something, or I'd tell 'em I have to go to the house, and I'd go and laugh as long as I wanted to, and I'd come back. You know, it hurts anybody when they're training if you laugh, so I didn't want to do that atall.

And they said, "Hicks, for gosh sakes, help!" Some of the rest of 'em, the kids, was just dying a-laughing, just laughing like crazy.

So I got in there and in about thirty minutes, I had the thing scraped, I mean, cleaned down and ready.

They said, "Now what are we gonna do?"

I said, "Put the gambreling stick in."

"What is a gambreling stick?"

"The thing you hang it up with. Hang it up in the cherry tree."

So I split the leaders and hung it up, and I said, "Boys, get 'er innards out."

"Gosh sakes!" they said, "We ain't a-gonna try that!"

So I took its innards out, you know. Cut its head off. Put 'em all in a tub. They was a-standin' there lookin' at it. One of 'em kept spittin', spittin', spittin'—you know, all that blood—spittin'.

I said, "Boy, that's a-lookin' pretty good, ain't it?" Directly, he went out through yonder holler, and I said, "Boy, you won't make no hog killer, will you?"

Well, I cut it down the back, and I said, "Boys, I'm through with it. You can take it and cut it up any way you want it now."

They said, "How are we gonna cut it?"

I said, "Well, just take it the way it is." I was done wore out with it then. Now, they was gonna butcher it theirselves.

And I told them—

they was all just about grown,

you know—

I said,

"Do anything that has to be done!

If you have to go out here and grub a tree,
grub it!
If you have to cut one down,
cut it!
If you have to dig up a half acre of ground,
dig it up!
If you have to lay a pipe from here to the barn,
go out and do it.
If you have to build a house or barn,
build it!
If you have to go out here and build you a mill,
do it."
"Gosh almighty, Hicks!"
they said,
"You've told us enough to do,
if we lived to be a hundred,
we'd never do it."
"Well,"
I said,
"That's what I've done."

Stanley Hicks, 1911 Watauga County

Dried Food

Dad, when he'd kill a beef, we'd dry it. He had a smoke house. He'd hang it up, keep a-smoking it and dry it. And then he had another one he built that we dried all of our vegetables in. We dried our apples in it, dried our beans in it, dried our pumpkins in it. Had shelves in it and then had a furnace under it.

Built a fire under it, and when the first shelf got dry, we'd change it, take it out and put it on the top. Take the top one out and put it down there.

Dried, maybe, a hundred pounds a week of pumpkin. Dried berries, blackberries, huckleberries, you know. Then Mother put 'em in a sack and hung 'em up. Put the pumpkin in a sack and hung it up. Put the what we call leather britches, these string beans, we'd string them up and hang them behind the stove.

We used hickory wood and corn cobs to dry the beef. See, we had soaked it in salty water maybe two days before we cured it. Take and pour it over it; then turn it. Then wipe it off. Lay it on a shelf on a white cloth to dry.

Just cut the beef up and hang it up by wires. Put the fire under it. Then the smoke cured it. Didn't have no floor in the smoke house. Just put a fire under it and smoked it.

When we got it smoked, we'd take what you make sheets out of, and we'd just sew that around there right tight. And that was it. And then when we wanted some, we'd just go and take 'er down; just strip 'er down and get what you wanted of it. Now, you could eat it just like it was or cook it, either one. We'd just eat it dry. We called it jerky. We had a knife that we could use to cut it with as thick as we wanted to. We didn't have to cook it.

I mean we young'uns would cut us off a piece of that jerky and put it in our pockets and go to cut hay. And we'd take our knife and cut us off some to eat. Boy! It was good! It was salty. Ready to go!

See, we run out tree sugar. Tap a tree. Bore a hole in a tree with a bit. Then drive a elder spout in there for the water to run out. Catch it in a trough. Carry it in and make tree sugar out of it. Boil it down, you know.

Then take the tree sugar and put it in these here biscuits. Take several of 'em, about a dozen of 'em, you know. Put it in there and when it dried, then take it and walk across the mountain to Elk Park and sell it for twenty-five cents a cake. You know, get a little money.

Stanley Hicks, 1911 Watauga County

A Step Stove

My mother wove a lot of clothes. She did all of her darning and knitting, knitted most of our socks and all of that stuff. She was a very working woman. She never, seemed like, was ever still.

Most of the time we got up between four and five o'clock in them days. Got up early. Of course, most people went to bed early in them days, too.

It was all oil lamps, you know. I remember the first stove we ever had in the place. Mother cooked on the fire, but we finally got a small stove, wood stove. I think it was what we called a "step stove" in that day. Had two different tops on it, separated. Had two burners down here, and two up here. And that was the first stove my mother ever had to cook on.

Add McMillan, 1889 Alleghany County

Barefoot in Summer

We bought the children's shoes, then,
just like we do now—
one pair a year, then.
And they went barefoot all summer.
But their feet would get so tough,
going barefooted,
that they
couldn't tell the difference
in the summer.

Iowa Patterson, 1881 Clay County

Black Bonnets

On Doe Hill there was what they called the Bonnet Split Mine. My grandmother wore bonnets, and they made the bonnets stand up with the splits of mica. They had little slits on the back side where they'd slip the splits in.

My grandfather tak'n me there when I was just six years old, but I couldn't find it now. He would always go there to get the mica for her bonnets. She wore the calico bonnets and the black bonnets. My mother, until she died, kept one of the black bonnets.

See, the older ones wore the black bonnets on Sunday, and the younger ones wore the calico with the different colored flowers and things. They also wore long skirts with ruffles on them. My grandmother always wore a white apron with a ruffle on it, too.

When I was baptized, I was one year old, and my grandmother wore a long dress with ruffles on it and a white apron. My mother has told me that many a time.

I was seventy-five the sixteenth of May [1979], and I made all my children's clothes, every one of them. My first four were girls, and I made all their clothes.

I've raised twelve children, and I've only lost one thirty-eight-year-old son. Twelve children.

Doctors used to have an awful lot of trouble getting to the homes in the wintertime. One of my daughters had bronchial pneumonia before there was anything to take care of that. That was before sulphur. Our old home doctor, Dr. Sloop, from up here at Crossnore, made thirteen trips and walked a mile from the top of the mountain down under the mountain to see her. We were a mile down on Brush Creek. He made thirteen trips to see her. She was four years old then.

But she's strong and well now. Lives in South Carolina and has her first grandchild. My great-grandchild. I've just got ten. And twenty-six grandchildren.

I think that's what makes you young—caring for children. It's the wonderfullest thing in the world.

Back then I did most of my sewing at night after I put my children to bed. Quilting. Things like that.

> But we told stories to the children.
> We enjoyed the children
> at night around the fireplace
> more than anything else
> in the world.
> And they could set still
> and listen
> then.
> They can't do that today.

Winnie Biggerstaff, 1904 McDowell County

Chapter 3. Child Life

With age, one's thoughts naturally gravitate to childhood, making this topic one of ready and easy recall. Inevitably, a twinkle lights up the narrator's eyes, and a slow smile mellows a furrowed face as he begins to relate beloved stories of "back when I was a child. . . ."

Just as adult life around the turn of the century demanded self-reliance, so did the lives of children. Early risings, long hours of field work, and home chores left relatively little time for play. Indeed, playtime was a luxury, often saved for weekends when the work was done.

Ingenuity was demanded from an early age, as children frequently made their own toys. Experience taught with a hard disciplinary hand, and schooling followed suit. As Stanley Hicks relates, "The hide flew!"

Was it any wonder that many children were practical jokesters and, consequently, were labeled "mean"? If entertainment was to be had, it, too, was self-made. However, honesty was a way of life, and respect for parents and elders was unquestioned. Since large families necessitated much cooperative effort, whatever Papa said was law!

Making Toys

We made our toys.
We made our little trucks,
made 'em out of wood.
Made our wagons that we played with.
We'd take a crosscut saw,
cut down a blackgum tree,
and we sawed our wheels out of it.
Made our wagons,
and we didn't have grease
like we have today
to make 'em run fast.

We'd take a fatback meatskin
and put around the axle,
and that'd make 'em really fly
off'n the hill.

If we ever had any free time, it'd be on Sunday. Sometimes we'd take these wagons and go out and clean up the side of a mountain, grub it out and make racetracks similar to what they have today, only we'd have 'em straight down the mountain.

Get all skint up once in a while, but nobody got hurt seriously.

And we had places on our raceway where we could pass, and if you were lucky, you got up enough speed to pass 'em, and if you didn't, you'd have a wreck. Might get hurt. Our mothers didn't worry about that.

And we played a lot in the trees like monkeys. We'd jump from one tree to another. Had grapevines to swing from. We'd just bail out of the top of a pine tree and maybe go two-thirds of the way down, you see, then catch the limbs with our hands to get away a lot of times. Playing fox and dog.

I used to go a-fishin' with my father on Sunday. And we didn't have fishing gear like they have today. We cut a poplar pole, got some string, and a lot of times didn't have a fishhook. We'd take a straight pin and bend it or either a safety pin and cut it off and make a fishhook.

We went down what they call "Ridge Mountain" over here one Sunday, and it was a-rainin' a little bit. I stayed about a hundred yards ahead of my father, always, because I knew when you got a mess of fish, it was all over.

This one particular time,
I was just having the best time
I'd ever had in my life
catching fish,
and Daddy,
he walked up on me and said,
"How many you got?"
I said,
"I don't know.
I got a pretty good bunch."
He wanted to know where they were,
and I told him.
We didn't have a string.
We just got a forked stick to put 'em on
and stuck 'em back in the water.
I told him,

and he went over there
and pulled 'em up.
He said,
"That's enough; that's a mess."

And if he'd just a-grabbed a limb
and whipped the blood out of me
and let me go on fishin',
I'd a-felt real good.
For I was a-havin' more fun fishin'
than I'd ever had in my life.

But, you see,
you didn't take more
than you could use.

   If you went a-rabbit hunting, you eat the rabbits. You didn't kill 'em
and leave 'em a-layin'; you dressed 'em, and they was cooked and put on
the table. And it was the same way with these fish. You'd get a mess,
and you didn't try to be a pig and take 'em all. You left some for the next
guy or another time to go back and catch 'em.

Ralph Crouse, 1922 Alleghany County

A Prankster

I used to nail
my sister's boyfriend's snowshoes
down to the floor
so when he went out to put 'em on,
he couldn't get 'em! Ha!
I used to be the kind
that would do mean, sneaking things
like that!

And then we had a hall rack
in the hall.
And he'd hang that fuzzy cap on it—
you know, that had flaps on it.

And I'd take it
and put flour in it
so when he pulled it down,
the flour would go in his face.
I was always into something!

Children used to do things like that
more than they do now.
We had to do things like that
if we had any entertainment.

Vastie Hensley, 1904 Yancey County

My Last Whipping

We had a world of geese in those days, and they made them featherbeds. Oh, we was always fixed to sleep warm; we never did sleep cold.

Now, us boys always slept upstairs, and my mother nearly always built the fire every morning downstairs. She'd get up first. And she'd build the fire in the living room there. And then she'd go in the kitchen and build a fire.

She cooked over a fire. Didn't know nothing about a stove then. Well, she'd cook her breakfast on the fire there. And she'd get that breakfast ready, and she'd come through and holler, "Breakfast! Everybody up!"

Well, she'd go back and put that breakfast on the table. And you'd better be there when she got done. She'd give you time, but now, boys, if you was a little lazy about it, you'd wish you hadn't been. My goodness alive! If you didn't get out of there in time, that big long hand . . . ! And she done that in raising all the family. She always got up first and built the fires.

My mother was a big, strong, stout woman. She was as stout as most any man. She lived to be up in eighty years old and raised all us children and sent us all out a-doing for ourselves a long time before she died. She was a wonderful woman.

Now, Father, he and Mother were married in '65, and he died in '84. He was just forty years old, but he was an awful strict disciplinarian. Now, the older girls were about eighteen, twenty years old, and the two older boys were great big boys. And he had those children all trained down, and they never parted from it much. Mother carried that discipline on. Now, he had certain rules and regulations. Say, if I wanted to go somewhere, I'd say, "Pappy, can I go a certain place?"

"No, Son, you can't go."

Well, if I went back and asked him the second time, I'd recollect it as long as I lived. Now, when he said anything, that was law and gospel. Well, the children learned that.

Now, I can recollect the last whipping he give me, and we'se setting on the porch. My grandpappy and me was setting there. The older children and our renter was up in the field hoeing corn. And they had a little girl about my size. They had to bring her out there and let her play under the shade of the apple tree. Well, I said, "Pappy, can't I go up yonder and play with Suzie this evening?"

And he said, "No, you can't go."

Well, I recollect very well. I went around back of the house, and I cried a while. But I wiped my eyes all out. I knowed better, but I says, "I'm gonna try him one more time." So I come around one more time. I says, "Pappy, can't I go up there and play with Suzie?"

"You can go right up there and get me a whip off of that beech tree."

And I never asked him anymore about going to play with Suzie. That's the last whipping he ever give me, the last one I ever recollect of. I was about four years old. That was about a year before he died.

Henley Crawford, 1879 Clay County

Our Education

When I growed up, Dad took us out there, and he said, "Now, boys, when you do anything, do it right." And if we didn't, my gosh, Son, the hide flew! I mean, the hide come off! We'd hoe corn or anything, and if it wasn't done right, we went back over it. That was our education. It was good! We thought it was bad then.

We'd make these old wooden bicycles to ride on. That's the only thing we had to ride on. Take blackgum and cut blackgum wheels off. Put the brakes on here like on a wagon. Had a thing across down here to set on. Had an old gray seed sack, you know, to put on. We'd buy great, long seed sacks to put the corn in. Had to take it from the field to the house.

So we got it on, and we didn't know it was a-draggin'. Didn't care much no way. And we'd come down off that mountain, and by the time we'd get to the house, the end of the sack would be drug out, and the corn would be gone. And Dad would beat heck out of us. Then we'd have to cut wood to pay for the sack. Cut up slabs and sell 'em.

See, we had to pay him *fifty*! He had to pay twenty-five cents for the sack, and we had to pay him fifty!

Stanley Hicks, 1911 Watauga County

Rolling Kegs

Yeah,
it took a whole lot of work
to make one keg of syrup.
We'd carry, us young'uns would carry it in.
And it'd go to sloshing in these barrels.
Kegs, you know?
It'd get to sloshing,
and it'd sometimes get us down.
And we rolled some off the mountain
one time.
Got too lazy to carry it.
And the stopper knocked out.
Run over a rock pile.
Lost it,
but my dad didn't know nothing of it.
If he'd knowed it,
he'd a-took the hide off of us.

He was plumb rough,
but he had to be, I guess.
Now,
back then,
the parents was good to the young'uns,
but when they told 'em to do anything,
they done it.
Now the young'uns tell the parents what to do.
Then,
when my dad told us to do anything,
we expected to do it.

What did he use to whip us with?
Anything he could get his hands on,
just to be fair with you.
That could be a belt
or anything he could get.
A piece of leather.
Most of the time it was his shaving strap.
Or else he just cut him off a birch switch
or whatever was closest.
We didn't think when he was doing it,
that it was right,
but now we appreciate every bit of it.
My mother wasn't too bad.
She was pretty rough sometimes, though.
There was several of us, you know.
And back then,
we was always fighting and going on.
You know how young'uns is.
But when he told us to do anything,
we done it.

Stanley Hicks, 1911 Watauga County

An Unfair Deal

When I was a kid, they'd say, "Big foot a-settin' in your face ever night, / A-sleepin' at the foot of the bed," and "Take a cold 'tater and wait." Now, that's a true song. I've been in that. Company would come here, the neighbors, and Mother and Dad would feed 'em the last, the best eatin' we had to show up, and we'd have to starve. Keep us whopped away from the table. I'd went and got stovewood to cook it; and Mother, if I got around, 'count of being dirty—me with little old short knee britches and that homemade blouse down over it—she was ashamed of us, you see, 'count of the way we was dressed.

We'd get around the eatin' table, even after we'd got the stovewood to cook it with, and she'd come around and slap me till I'd see stars! And we'd have to wait. Then when we would go back, what little they had fixed, the best, they'd eat it all up.

And I'd always go to grumbling about it 'cause I's the one who got the stovewood. They ought to put a little away for me. Kept it back. And she'd say she didn't think. So I'd say, "Think next time." It was an unfair deal. I'd worked. Now, the other young'uns, it didn't hurt them, but I'd worked. Got the stovewood and packed it.

You had to pack the wood in on your back. Chop with an old dull axe. Didn't even have a file, grindin' stone, or nothing to sharpen it with. Dad didn't. But the others did now, had them crank grinding stones. After I got bigger, older, I'd go down to my grandfather's and help him grind his. Crank it for him, and he'd help grind mine. Made it easier on me.

Ray Hicks, 1922 Watauga County

A Newcomer

I never been in this county
but thirty-two year.
I lived in Macon County.
I don't even know all the people here yet.
I've just been here thirty-two year.

I learned to spin
when I was eight year old.

I had to climb in a chair
to band the wheel.
It'd throw the band
once in a while.
So I'd climb up in a chair
and put that band back around that big wheel.

I learned to milk, now,
when I was eight year old.
Shear sheep when I was eleven year old.

Tennie Cloer, 1886 Cherokee County

A Narrow Escape

I can remember my brother dropping my sister in the fire when I was just four years old. He stumped his toe on the hearth. Our mother and daddy were making homemade syrup.

And so I was too little to be handling her, you know, and she went in the fire. And they was away making syrup — well, it was half a mile back to the place.

So I run every step of the way and told them that my sister was burning. I thought she was. And it was cold.

But my brother, now, he was four year older than me. And she was the one just younger than me. We were just children. Had a big fire.

Well, it burnt her clothes off, but my brother got her out. And my mother, she come. Now, she raised these great, big beets. Big as a half-gallon bucket.

So she ran out and pulled up one, scraped it, and bound that to her hand. That took the fire out.

Tennie Cloer, 1886 Cherokee County

Pea Time

Children used to make playhouses.
Well,
they just played anything to pass the time.
They weren't restless like children today.
Why,
children now don't know what they want.

Started to school in September.
Went six weeks.
Then pea time would come.
Pea time.
We had to stop and pick peas.
And pull fodder off'n the stalks for the cows.
You'd stop for two or three weeks.
Then you'd go back the rest of them months.
We went to school four months in all.

Nannie Smith, 1888 Clay County

School Life

When I went to school, they had it four months. I went to a little old log school, log house. Well, it burnt up, and then they built another one. And when we went to school, we walked. We waded in snow knee deep. If it rained, we come through it.

We cut our own wood with crosscut saws and had heating stoves in the room. And the pipe would go plumb through, you know. And we cut our own wood and carried it in there and built our own fire. If we didn't do it, the teacher showed us how to do it with a good, long, keen switch! But us young'uns was used to it at home, and it didn't bother us.

The ground squirrels then would bury chestnuts. They call 'em chipmunks; we call 'em ground squirrels. And they'd bury around a half-a-bushel to a bushel in a hole. And when fall would come, we'd take a mattock and a shovel and go dig 'em out. And then we'd take all these chestnuts and sack 'em up and take 'em home and dry 'em and eat 'em, you see. Find 'em in the squirrel's beds.

So I got me one and was digging up chestnuts on my way to school one day. And I come to the ground squirrel in his bed asleep. Well, I caught him and took him to the schoolhouse, tied him up in a handkerchief Mother had made me. You know, you could breathe through it.

So I put it in my desk. And it kept whipping around in there till it got out, you know. It come out and got in that schoolhouse, and here it went!

Well, we was in the woman teacher's room then. We'd go in there, and she'd teach the smaller grades, and then the man would teach us the others. Well, we was in there that time, and it got loose. Ha!

Just to tell you the truth, it was just terrible bad! You know, she had this big, long dress on, and the ground squirrel went under it. Went in down there [bottom] and came out up here [back of the neck]! Us kids was getting a kick out of it! There was a knothole in the ceiling of the schoolhouse, and it went in the knothole. And it would come out, stick its head out, and we'd throw a eraser at it.

Well, we got whipped awful bad off of it. We never did get our ground squirrel. It stayed in there.

And them teachers, Son, I'm telling you when they told you anything, they just whipped the hide off of you if you didn't do like they said. Then they'd take you up to the blackboard and make you a mark, and you'd have to stand with your nose up agin it, you know, ever so long.

I thought the teacher had been a little rough with me; well, he whipped me over things he shouldn't. Young'uns would jump on me, and I couldn't help it, so I just had to beat the heck out of 'em. And then he'd whip me over that. But I didn't start it.

So I would tell him, but that didn't do no good. I got a whipping just the same. So I got studying and studying how to get even with him.

Well, I decided to get a hornets' nest and put it up over the door. Plug it, and when he went in at the door—he was pretty tall—he would knock it out with his head, and they would just sting the heck out of him.

So I went, took my handkerchief—and it was pitch dark—put my handkerchief over the nose of the hornets' nest. And then I got the hornets' nest down and put me a plug in the end of it.

Well, I went on to the schoolhouse. I went to the door, but he had locked the door, so I couldn't get in. So I went and raised the window. Went in and put it right over the door right where his head would hit it.

Big hornets' nest. And it was full! Put it right where he'd hit it at. Then I went back home. Mother and Dad—didn't nobody know nothing about it! See—it was on a little limb, and I just pushed that limb back in the crack.

Next morning he lined us up. Every young'un, now, had to line up behind the teacher and follow him in. So I didn't crowd in, you know, to get next to the teacher. I'd been a-doin' it, gettin' in there, but I stayed way back.

Well, he unlocked the door, and when he went in, he just tore the thing up! And the house looked black! Gosh, he commenced fightin', and the young'uns a-fightin'! He didn't know what had happened, but he come out that door saying, "God bless you, get out of here quick!" Said, "The devil's in the house!"

So we didn't have no school that day. I mean, we got out of it! Every kid went home.

Oh, he was so mad the next day. He went to the doctor, you know. Old country doctor. Went and got some medicine and put on him and went back. And he looked about like a scarecrow—his eyes, you know.

And he went in, and he said, "All you young'uns, all you young'uns, come up here on the stage. We all got up there. There was about thirty-three of us, all lined up in three groups. Got the biggest behind and on down the list.

And the hornets had left. They'd got 'em out of there. And he said, "Now, then, I want to know which one of you young'uns done it."

Well, it'd a-been a blamed fool to tell it.

So he said, "Did you do it?" to the bigger ones.

"No."

"Did you do it?"

"No."

On down the line. I's in the second row. He was takin' out the bigger ones first, comin' on down. Come to me, and he said, "Did you do that?"

I said, "How would I have got 'em up there? I'd a-been stung to death, worse than you are." I said, "I don't fool with them things. I'm scared of 'em, myself." Just big talk, you know. So he went on down the line. Never questioned me anymore a-tall; just went on down the line.

He said, "I know who done it. That Airy Masten done it, and I'm going after him."

See, Airy Masten was about out of school, and the teacher had whipped him, and Airy had cussed him.

Well, the teacher went up there to see his daddy and got with Airy and his daddy. Talked to them. And they run him off. They got the gun and run the teacher off. They told him to get out.

Well, it went on and went on. School was gettin' out, way up late in the fall of the year. Oh, yeah, he kept teachin' school.

So one day he said, "I'd give a hundred dollars to find out who put that hornet's nest up there."

"Well," I said, "if you'll give me the hundred dollars, I'll find it out."

"Well," he said, "you'll have to find out before."

I said, "No, I'll have to have the hundred dollars first."

He said, "Why?"

"Because when I find out and tell you," I said, "they're gonna kill me. And if I don't have it first, the hundred dollars won't do me no good."

He said, "I won't give you nothing. You don't know who done it."

I said, "No, if I knowed who done it, I'd tell you."

And then one time we went to school, and we had a girl there. She was awful — you know how some tongue-tattlers is. She'd run to school and tell everything these boys done. So me and my brother, my oldest brother, we's a-goin' to school. And she run on ahead and told what we'd done. We hadn't done anything, you know.

So when we went in, the teacher got us up on the stage. And I said, "Well, now, before you whip us, you go back up there and ask the folks if she told you what we done to 'em. I said, "She ain't nothing but a damn lie."

Well, they whipped me over saying "damn."

So me and my brother, we said we'd get even with 'em. Then the teacher went back up there and asked about us. They told him, "We ain't never seed the boys do nothing. They've always been nice over here."

See, she didn't like us because we was gettin' more up in the grades than she was. So I told my brother, I said, "If she keeps that up, we'll get her."

Well, she went down through there one day, and we heard her hollering. So we run down there to help her out and see what was the matter. She was just a-puttin' on, you see. And then she made out to them that we was a-beatin' on her. So they could hear her hollering, and the teacher whipped us for it.

So I says, "Just wait. Just wait till tomorrow evening, Friday evening, when we get out of school." I says, "If she wants to cry, she'll be glad to cry!"

She was up about grown. So we was going along the next day, my brother and me, and we had to cross this old nailed-up fence. You know, some was laid up, and some was nailed up. This fence had a nailed-up crossing place.

So I went ahead of her. Went just as hard as I could go and got ahead of her, so when she crossed over, I could just bend her over the fence and he could just burn her up.

So, when I got there, I just grabbed her by the hair of the head and pulled her down over the fence, and I said, "Now, Floyd, give it to her." And gosh, he got ahold of her and he blistered her hind end, and it popped! They heard it plumb to the house. He raised the whelps! I mean they was that long, as big as your hand.

And I mean she went home a-crying. I mean she was really a-screamin'.

And I said, "Now we'll catch it a-Monday."

But do you know what? She went back to school on Monday, and she never opened her mouth about that! And she never did tell another lie on us what time we went to school. Best friend we had.

And then we got into it one day. Going to school one day when it was pretty cold, pretty bad. Had two mill ponds. We had one that was ground in, and then John Mast that I was tellin' you about, he had one.

So we was going by there and got into a fight. My younger brother, they was about to kill him. I wouldn't bother 'em as long as he was winnin'. Long as he won, that was okay. Then here come three or four of 'em like flies.

Here come one at me, and I dodged him. But he fell, and when he fell, I just took and grabbed him by his hind legs and drug him in the mill pond. Just drug him backwards, you see. And I mean soaked him, plumb up, but didn't get his head in it.

So he went on to school with that mud and stuff on him, and, my gosh, you talk about catchin' a beatin', I got it! They whipped me till it was pitiful.

And then I went one time — we's a-givin' Christmas presents away — that was the funniest thing! You know, everybody takes something to the teacher and gives him.

So Daddy had killed some hogs, and we'd scraped the tails. Killed an old sow, and her tail was about twelve or fourteen inches long. A great, big long one. And I fixed it real nice and all, cleaned it off real good and all. Wrapped it up in paper. Put this Christmas paper on it and put the teacher's name on it. Never put mine on it, but I took it on down and put it under the Christmas tree.

Didn't let nobody see it. I slipped it out of my pocket and threw it under the Christmas tree.

Oh, we's around there gettin' our presents and all. Teacher, he was so glad! "Boy," he said, "they really thought of me. Here's the best one."

Somebody said, "What do you think it is?"

He said, "I'll bet that's a big, long stick of peppermint candy." You know, you've seen 'em that long.

Well, he opened up that hog tail. Ha! You talk about the young'uns a-beatin' and laughin' and screamin' and hollerin'! He looked at it a long time, dropped it down, and said, "Well, it will make some soup." It was fixed nice, you know.

Stanley Hicks, 1911 Watauga County

Starting Over Every Year

I was at school one day, and they'd made a rule not to go after water, out to the spring, without leave. And I wasn't there, and I come back the next day, and so I got a bawlin' out.

Well, my cousin and I had a table up on the rostrum that went all across the back end of the school house. And so the next day I brought a bucket and a dipper. And I filled my bucket full of water and set it up on the table. And every little bit, I'd have to drink some water.

When students misbehaved back then, they whipped 'em. Whipped 'em with what they called a "shonny haw." That was just a long switch with no limbs off of it or anything—just a long switch.

When my brother and a neighbor boy got in a fight, the teacher, to punish them, he made them whip each other. And they whipped hard. I guess they wasn't friends for a while.

We had only three months of school. And so we got over so far in our books, and then school was out. Then the next year, they started us in the front of the book again. And so we never got any further in the book, each year, than we had gone the year before.

We just had a one-room schoolhouse, about fifty or sixty students, and one teacher.

Ruth Sturgill, 1893 Alleghany County

Grubbing Stumps

Back in those days, if you got into meanness at school, if you didn't get a whipping, well, they had stumps to grub at recess and at lunch hour. So they'd put you out a-grubbin' and stay out there with you and wouldn't let you play any.

It was either that or get a whipping, and most of us had rather get out there and grub a big oak stump than get a whipping.

We'd get a mattock and a shovel and just start digging around 'em. And then, when you got 'em out, the teacher would help you. Take rails or long poles and prize 'em out. Then you'd roll 'em down in the gully if there was one down there and fill up the hole and grass it over.

It's a lot of hard work. Takes some time, but I've helped clean up a lot of ground that way. 'Course, it was hard work, but we didn't mind it. Back then, you didn't mind working. You didn't mind walking five or six miles to work.

Ralph Crouse, 1922 Alleghany County

Playing Fox and Dog

I was seven years old at the time we moved over there and started school at Bethel in the wood house on a little old knoll. I was coming seven when we went over there. Next fall I started at school.

And up in this Pick-Breeches, now, there was a lot of rough boys. It was pretty rough, and I was teached to be calm, you know, by my mother. Well, Dad did, too, but not as much as my mother.

And so some of the boys right above the church in there, where that pine is yet, some of these boys from Pick-Breeches said, "Let's stay out of school and play fox and dog." They used to play that back then. One would be a fox and the others, the dogs. And, gosh, they'd run 'em all over them mountains, treeing 'em, and trying to catch 'em. Some boys would climb a tree, like the fox, or jump off'n a cliff before they'd be caught and nearly get killed by the dogs.

Well, I said, "But I'm afeared it'll be found out, and the teachers will whop me." And I said, "I'll just go on to school."

They said, "You'll tell on us!"

But I said, "No, I won't tell on you."

And so at dinnertime, about dinnertime, they'd lost their mind, a-runnin' the fox, and got to barkin' so till the teacher heared 'em. They forgot where they was at. They got carried away with their game, a-playin' that fox and dog, and the teacher heared 'em, three or four of 'em. So the teacher went up in there and got 'em, brought 'em in at dinner, the recess at dinner, right at the last of it. So they jumped on me that evening and come near a-killin' me. I said, "They just heared you. I never told on you." But they beat me till I couldn't walk.

Now, when they caught the fox, they just growled and chewed him up a little bit, like a dog. They wouldn't carry it too fer. Some would a-killed 'em, but the others would get 'em to quit, you know. Some would get carried away and get rough, would chew 'em up, beat 'em up—you see, a dog would kill a fox! They'd say, "We're supposed to kill him just like a dog kills a fox." Some would say that, but the others would keep 'em down.

Ray Hicks, 1922 Watauga County

Stinkbase

You know, back in those days, we'd go to school. And the main thing at school was baseball—or townball—we called it town-ball. We played lots of townball at school. And then we played a game we called "stinkbase."

Well, we'd choose up and have two sides: one over here, and one over there. And they'd have a place here they called the stinkbase. Say, me and my crowd over here, we'd venture agin one another, and we'd break out and run.

And I'd catch one of that crowd over there, and I'd bring him and put him in the stinkbase. He had to stay there. And they'd catch one of us, and they'd take him and put him in their stinkbase. See, they had a stinkbase, too. Well, we'd play backwards and forwards like that until we saw which one had the most in their stinkbase, you know.

Well, we had, say, three or four over here. Now, if one of theirs could slip around and get one of these, he'd take him home. But now, you had to be sharp if you got 'em. And while you was getting 'em, they'd like to catch you and put you in.

Well, after a while, they'd go to crying, "We wish you'd come and get these. They're stinking so bad we can't stand 'em."

Henley Crawford, 1879 Clay County

Riding a Schoolwagon

We had to walk about two miles to school.
And when the weather was very, very bad,
my mother would drive a covered wagon
and pick up all the children
from our area
and drop them off at their homes,
and we'd be the last ones on the route.
We all just crawled in and rode together
and had a good time going home.

She would drive horses,
and it was the bow type covered wagon,
you know,
with the sloping ends.
They called them schooners.
They had the cloth covers over them.
They were made of very heavy cloth
similar to canvas.

And we didn't get wet in them.
Usually,
there was straw in it,
and we'd sit on the floor,
just like a haystack!

Mildred Torney, 1918 Alleghany County

A Light to Study By

When I went to school, a lot of times we'd run out of kerosene and didn't have any kerosene to have a light at night. And it was a long ways to the store, so we'd get these pine knots and split them and stick them up in the fireplace there to make a light to see how to get your lesson at night. Made a good light, but it was a little smoky. You got a lot of smoke from it. That's the biggest thing. If you got that in your eyes, it'd burn. And you had to sit up right close to the fireplace.

That was just in case you run out of kerosene, and a lot of times you'd run out and it'd be cold and rough, and you couldn't get to go to the store and get any for four or five days.

Ralph Crouse, 1922 Alleghany County

A Teacher Recalls

We went to school in the grades only about a half a mile. So we didn't ride a horse. We walked. And then in high school, I went to Andrews. Went on the train on Monday morning and came home on Friday afternoon. Had to board. We had no high schools. Murphy had a high school, but the train went toward Andrews. So my brother and I went to Andrews. Had two sisters that finished in Murphy. Then I went away to school.

Then I taught fifty years. The first year I taught, I got thirty-five dollars a month. And I had what they called then the first-grade certificate. And that was my salary. But then the next year, I went on, and I think I got fifty dollars that year.

When I got a hundred dollars a month, I thought I'd reached the top.

But the work was entirely different then from what it is now. I always taught in a graded school, so I just had one grade.

For two or three years
we had no lunchrooms.
And the room was heated with a big stove.
So I suggested to the children
if they'd bring vegetables,
we'd make soup on our stove.
And every fellow brought his own dish.
And his spoon.

And every morning
we'd put on a pot of water,
put in our vegetables,
and have hot soup at lunch.
And then we'd put on a pot of water
and wash our dishes.
Scald them.

Certain days certain girls
peeled potatoes,
washed 'em,
put 'em in.
Or tomatoes.
And sometimes we'd have a piece of beef
we'd put in.
We'd put that on early.

And we have a minister here in the county who was talking not long ago about how good that soup was that we'd have for our lunch. It would smell good all morning. Made you good and hungry.

Kate Hayes, 1892 Cherokee County

Chapter 4. Of Work

Mountain men were hard pressed to find enough work to earn livable wages. While the land in the rest of the state was suitable for farming, mountain land was steep and inaccessible, and the distance to market often made selling the crop unprofitable. Usually farming meant producing enough corn and grain to keep a family going—a hardy garden and a few hogs.

Work was where one could find it. And that could mean walking long distances. When the lumber companies came in, bringing with them the need for the building of roads and rails to transport logs and lumber out of the highlands, mountain men flocked out of the hills, some walking for hours each day to the lumbering or road-building sites.

Eventually the virgin timber was practically exhausted, but the roads and rails remained to provide routes to markets. Thus, in certain areas, the quarrying of marble and the mining of feldspar, mica, and iron gave some relief to the mountaineer in search of work.

In the meantime, being the industrious individual he was, the mountain man turned to tanning, with its demand for tanbark; milling; or blacksmithing to hold his family together. Bartering was common practice, and both goods and services were swapped back and forth. It was not uncommon to work all day for "a hatful of corn."

Getting By

You had to do something back then to live, to survive. There was no jobs. The first job that come in our country was Cranberry Mine, out here at Elk Park. The old copper mine out at Cranberry. That was the first job ever in this country.

Later, me and my wife married in 1933. WPA come in, and I worked two years for seventy-five cents a day on it. Then I worked for two years for a dollar a day. Now, I mean we lived, but we just did get by. Back then, people didn't raise tobacco. The first Dad raised, he got seven cents a pound for it. Had to take it to Johnson City, stay down there a week to get to sell it. He'd get somebody to haul it down there in a old A-Model truck.

See, when I growed up, the roads were built with free labor. Didn't get no money for it. They'd work about a day a week, about four days a month, to keep the roads up. And I'd go carry water. Always when Dad went to work, I'd go carry water. Made a hand, you know. And I'd take old rails and prize the sled runners over rocks. Had a yoke of steers, you know.

But we lived and made out. Dug our ground up with old eye-hoes. Got one up in the shop now. Sort of like a mattock, you know, but we called 'em eye-hoes. And we'd dig up the ground with it.

We'd get a yoke of cattle, get 'em broke till we could work 'em, and then Dad would have to sell 'em to get a little money. Twenty-five dollars for a yoke of cattle. Yeah, that was oxen. They would turn in the yokes and stuff. They was aggravating.

Then we'd have to go digging the ground up. There was several of us there—nine or ten. About nine got grown. Nine children. And several of us boys would work like that. But we made out and lived. If it was to get back that way now, people couldn't live.

Stanley Hicks, 1911 Watauga County

The Groundhog Thresher

The first threshing machine I ever saw, they called it a ground-hog thresher. We raised wheat and rye for our bread, you know. Now, rye bread was really good. Yes, it was! Well, the thresher would come, and everyone around in the whole country around would just go with it. And they'd help one another until it was all done. And then they'd have dinner or supper, one, whichever it was.

The way they made that thresher: it was a big square thing, about six feet every way. And there were six horses hitched to it. Them horses went around and around it. And they stepped so many steps (I don't remember how many steps that was), but as they stepped them steps, that turned that thing, that machine, under there.

And the faster the horses went, the faster the thing run. And that wheat came out, and they caught it in a big place under there. They caught it in half-a-bushels, and they poured it into a hopper that they had. Then the men turned this around here and cleaned the wheat all out. The wind would blow all the chaff away and clean the wheat out. That was something to see—the groundhog thresher.

Now, they cut the wheat with a cradle, you know, a great big thing with fingers out. About six or eight fingers. And they moved the thresher from one place to another as they cut the wheat.

They had it to take down, too. And it was a lot of trouble to take it down.

Iowa Patterson, 1881 Clay County

Building Fences

The chestnut trees was used for rails for fences; and, of course, there was wormy chestnut lumber. Now we don't have that. So many things we don't have.

I remember my father-in-law when he first moved to Brush Creek. He was a person who believed in doing things the hard way. He came down one morning, and I had two children at that time. Said, "What do you intend doing today?"

I said, "Well, I guess I'll find something."

He said, "How about helping me build a fence?"

Well, I picked up the children and carried them over there and let my mother-in-law care for them. And so, instead of cutting the trees down up on top of the hill where he was building the fence, he cut them down underneath, and it took two of us to carry a rail to the top to put on his fence. He had no reason for it that I knew of except that he found the straighter trees down there. They weren't as straight up on top of the hill. And he had to have straight trees to make rails!

Now, he sawed them the length with the crosscut saw that he wanted 'em, and then they took iron wedges and a maul made out of wood and split those rails. Chestnuts split easy, real easy. And they last a long time.

Now, he didn't build a six-rail fence; he built a ten-rail fence. And there couldn't anything get out of where he built his fences.

Winnie Biggerstaff, 1904 McDowell County

Good Clean Work

Well,
I went to the mountain
with a saw, hammer, axes, and wedges
to help cut the logs
to prepare to haul to the sawmill
to help make lumber out of.

It was a band mill.
Well,
they used this lumber
in building ships
along through World War I
on up to World War II.
And I was only seventeen
and eighteen years old
in them days.
But I followed that
on up till about ten years ago.

It was good work.
Good, clean work.
We had nice beds to sleep on at night.

You'd lay down tired and sleep good.
Good food to eat.
Good water to drink.
Had a camp where we eat, slept,
you know, in there.
Pure water to drink.

We all was healthy.
Didn't have no doctor with us.
We just went on and worked.
If anybody got cut with the axe
or saw,
why,
we'd take him in and put him
on a flatcar
on the railroad.

Had a train to haul these logs to the mill,
and if anybody got cut or hurt,
they'd put him on a platform
and haul him out
down to the band mill.
Then they'd get a doctor to see him,
patch him up, you know.
Patch him up and let him go
till he got well.
So when he got well,
he'd come back,
and they'd let him have his job back.

Burnie Higgins, 1903 Yancey County

Huge Timber

Back in the thirties, the Linville Lumber Company run a spur line from what they called McCanless Gap. It's Invershill now. And we built a railroad across and under the Sugar Mountain toward where the ski slopes are at now, in the Norwood settlement.

We was grading for the railroad to be laid down, and there was a lot of virgin pine, timber. Hemlocks that was anywhere from seven to eight

feet through at the bottom. We would dig around it and let the whole thing fall down instead of cutting through it. Then we'd saw it in two and roll the stump out, too.

Dig around the roots. Cut the roots off. Get it close. And it was much easier to get it up thataway than to cut the timber and then blast it out.

That's a much easier way. Why, those trees, goodness sakes, they were two hundred feet tall. Hemlocks. Course, there was a lot of other timber there, too, but the pine, the hemlock, was the largest. There was birch; there was beech, maple, all kinds of different woods. Now, maple, we hit some large trees of maple, but the pine was the largest.

Then they built a railroad over into there and got the most of that out. And the Linville Company ran; oh, it was a boom town for a long time. And then, after all that timber was out, the mill shut down, and people started going to other places, looking for other ways to find jobs. Course, it's still a summer resort.

Doyle I. Oakes, Sr., 1909 Avery County

Coming Up the Hard Way

And we lived,
I'd say,
very poor.
Hard-up.
I come up the hard way.
If they come up any harder
than we did,
well,
you don't see 'em around much.
They didn't make it.

George Perkins, 1916 Mitchell County

Logging Camp

This story about McMillan happened in 1908, down on the Little Tennessee in North Carolina. I went down there with a fellow by the name of Vaught and got a job in a logging camp.

And there were quite a few mountain boys working there and a lot of Cherokee Indians, too. But I hadn't been there but a little bit till I saw a fellow by the name of Bill Broche that was a-workin' in the same camp. He was a foreman on the log train. He had worked with my brother one time in West Virginia, and I knew him well.

He thought he was a good logger. And he took a notion he wanted me on that log train. So he went to another fellow by the name of Vaught, a brother to the man I went down there with. He was the general superintendent there. And he told him he wanted me on the log train.

Vaught said, "He's too young a man. I can't put him on. You'll get him hurt."

Broche told him, "No, I'll take care of him." And nothing doing, but Broche put me on that train as a tong hooker. So I taken the job and went out with Broche and worked with him several weeks. I worked loading logs. I was the tong hooker for the log train.

Our log loader was a man by the name of Doug Glistenbee. The engineer was Sid Aldman. And the man I went down there with, Vaught, he took the job of firing the train, firing the engine. So we made up the train group.

And we'd go up that creek on that railroad, and the logs would be dumped off that mountain into the creek, and I'd have to go into the creek with the tongs and hook 'em all so they could load 'em onto the train.

So I worked there quite a bit; and, finally, the boys up in that camp got some of that mountain liquor and got to drinking too much.

And so the general superintendent came in there and found it out, and he said they'd have to stop it. If they didn't, he'd have to fire any man that wasn't able to go out on the job on Monday morning.

So, Bill Broche, my train foreman, was pretty bad to get drunk on weekends. And we knew that he'd be about the worst fellow — that he might get fired. So, one Monday morning, sure enough, Bill come up missing. And Vaught come over there for me and him to take out the train.

We waited a while, and Bill didn't show up, so we went out with the train that day. And he was on the top loadin' 'em, and I was working the tongs.

And, along in the evening, he says to me, he says, "Mac, I'll have to give you Bill's job."

I says, "No, I can't handle it, Wylie."

"Oh," he says, "you can. I'll help you out, and it won't be long till you'll be able to load these logs."

Went on, a little later in the evening. He hadn't said nothing, and I says to him, I says, "Wylie, you know something?"

He said, "What?"

I said, "Bill Broche can stay drunk three days a week, and then he'll get more logs out of this mountain than any other man you've got."

And he jabbed his hook down on a log and said, "You're damn right!" He says, "He ain't gone yet."

And that night when we come in, Bill was there. Still drinking. And he met me as I come into the headquarters. Said, "Mac, I'm fired, ain't I?"

I said, "I don't know. I don't know yet."

And we went on, and after supper in the big room we was all sitting around and talking, and the superintendent come in. He sat around a little bit and said to Bill, says, "Bill, let's you and me talk a little." And he took him outside. And they talked.

And finally Bill come back in and looked at me and grinned. And I knew it was all over.

So Bill went back on the job.

And I stayed there after that, and Christmas was coming up, and a lot of the boys wanted to go home.

And, along at Christmastime, Bill went out, too. Then Vaught come to me and says, "Mac, would you like to work some during Christmas?"

I says, "I might as well. I'm not going home."

Then he says, "I'll tell you what I'll do. I'll give you the keys to the barn and all the outbuildings here, and you can take care of the camp during Christmas. You'll get your wages right on."

And I says, "All right. I'll take it." So I had the keys to all the places around, and everybody went out, nearly, except one fellow by the name of Dan Cable. He was a mountaineer, lived in what they called the Shuckstack Mountain district down there. And he was quite a hunter. Fisherman, too.

So Dan come to me, and he says, "Mac, you've got the keys to that powder house over there, haven't you?"

I says, "Yes, I have."

So he says, "Tell you what I'll do. If you'll go over there and steal me out a stick of dynamite and a couple of caps and a little fuse, me and you'll eat fish for Christmas."

I says, "All right, I'll do that."

So I went and got the dynamite for him and the caps, and he went off down on the Tennessee River. And he come back after a little while with a gunny sack and about all he could carry of the prettiest bluecats you ever saw. Bluecat fish.

Well, we cleaned them fish, and we sure eat fish for Christmas.

See, he'd just lit that dynamite fuse, threw it in the water, and blasted 'em out. It just killed 'em, and then you can just pick 'em up, you know. You shoot 'em and just knock 'em crazy. Kill 'em, and they come to the top.

So we had fish for Christmas, and I stayed on till next spring, pretty late, and I came home and knocked around the rest of that year up till 1909. And then I took a notion to go west.

Add McMillan, 1889 Alleghany County

A Campaign Promise

You know, back then they had free labor. There was an old colonial law that was in effect. Back when I was about grown. But I wasn't old enough. You had to be twenty-one to work on the road.

I remember, I was working for my brother. And a man came along riding a horse. He said his name was John Henry Tipton.

He was running for representative. He said, "I'll tell you fellers something; if you vote for me and help me go to Raleigh, you won't be giving this free labor no more."

And all them men said they'd vote for him. Well, he won. And when he got in, we never did have to do that no more. Yeah, he went to Raleigh. Everybody voted for him.

And about that time, it wouldn't have been long till I would have been old enough to work on them roads myself. That time he come along, I was working in my brother's place. I could do that, you know.

This man got my brother to work at his sawmill. And my brother said to me, "I'll give you a dollar a day to work in my time." I think he was making a little more than that at the sawmill. So I worked in his place. On the road.

No, I didn't think that road work was too hard. Cleaning out Ford's Creek where the wagons would go through. You'd get in there, pull your shoes off and clean Ford's Creek out. Fill up where it was routed out. It wasn't too hard.

Now, them roads, there was places, just a lot, where two couldn't pass. Just certain places they'd get to that they could pass. That was in wagons.

Pulled them wagons with horses. Sometimes have two teams when they had a big wagon load. See, it was a uphill pull. Why, there was one bank over there that was so steep that even when the cars went to running, they couldn't make it up there without being pushed or pulled.

Yeah, them men, they called them "overseers," you know, overseers over the road. They'd tell you when to come in, what time, where to work.

And everybody would take their dinner with them. When it come time to eat, they'd just set down and eat. Neighbors would be there, too. See, there'd be a big gang. Work a certain day, certain place.

We had one place back out on the mountain where just one man lived. And they'd go back in there to work on the road. You see, the mail went on horseback. Oh, them were bad roads then. He'd go up the mountain, be gone all day from the post office.

Harvey J. Miller, 1909 Mitchell County

It Was Just Live or Die!

Well, they come into Butler down here from Johnson City, and they built the railroad from Butler, that little old railroad plumb into Beech, where this project was at. I helped lay that steel all the way up through there and drive the spikes.

And so I worked two years there for a dollar a day. I walked ten miles. Twenty miles a day. Walked ten there and ten back.

Well, I'd leave home at four o'clock that morning and get there at seven. Started working at seven, worked to six o'clock at night. Then it would take me till nine o'clock to get home.

It was in the wintertime, and my clothes, with it snowing and all, would get wet and freeze into ice. When I come home and took 'em off and set 'em up agin the fire, they'd stand up!

That's the truth! It ain't nothing but the God's truth! It was just live or die. That was the only way we had to go.

And,
you know,
we had these trestles down here,
when I was walking,
and I fell through the trestle
into the river
in February
and wet me,
I mean, plumb up.
Fell down through it
'fore daylight.
Couldn't see
and stepped on a slippery place
where it was ice.
Went on to where I was a-workin' at
and built me up a fire.
Pulled my overalls off,
wrung 'em out,
dried 'em out,
put 'em back on,
and worked all day.

Stanley Hicks, 1911 Watauga County

No Time for Picnics

Used to be an old railroad station
in Doughton.
That's where the railroad come to.
That's where they brought
the fertilizer to.
And that's where they loaded the lumber on.

Didn't have no picnics there then.
Didn't have time for picnics.

Tom Pruitt, 1904 Alleghany County

Marble

There was not any public works much, back at that time. The quarry. Marble quarry. They had a marble quarry at Regal. Opened about, I guess, 1912.

And they shipped marble. They later made a finishing plant where they finished the stones and shipped out. That gave a number of people work.

They had one at Regal, and then they moved one to Marble. And that's still in operation.

Kate Hayes, 1892 Cherokee County

Digging Iron Ore

The Cranberry Iron Ore Mines operated over here. Oh, it was a boom town! We lived there around 1912, '13, '14, '15, '16, I guess, to '17 and '18. Then we moved back to the place where my home is now, in Newland.

Now, the iron ore, they worked it out in the tunnels. They had to blast it. They had to drill through the hard rock to put dynamite in it, and blast it out.

Then they would beat it up with hammers and load it. Bring it out in cars, load it into other cars, and send it to Johnson City, Tennessee.

It was kind of a brilliant-like dark black rock. Heavy. Very heavy. They'd just break it up till they could handle it and put it into cars. The furnace was over in Johnson City, you know. And then they'd melt it down.

Those mines went deep. Straight back into the side of the mountain. The mountain would be three, four, five hundred feet high, and they started down here. Went level a ways, maybe a little grade, or a downgrade.

At one time there was a pretty good number of people in Cranberry, but now they've all left out. There are a few of the oldtimers still there.

Now, these weren't like coal-mining people. Now, coal-mining people, you get a variety of different kind of people. These here were a more gentle type of people. Biggest majority of them were from out of Avery County. A few come in from other counties.

At that time, I don't know, they probably made ten cents an hour, a dollar a day.

Now, there was not much danger. See, they had such hard rock. The only thing they had to watch would be loose rocks a-hanging overhead. But they kept people going with a bar, a-gouging them and bringing 'em down.

But they did have some explosions in there. And my brother-in-law, Frank February, he got blowed up in there, but he lived for quite a while. Some of the pieces went into his head and around his skull, and he died from that.

It seemed that the explosion was caused because when they set it off to fire, it didn't go off at the time that they thought it would, so they went back in to check it and see what was wrong, and it blew up. I believe there were three killed at that time.

We had spar—feldspar—and mica mined here, too. You see, Avery County and Spruce Pine and through Mitchell County also had it; and, actually, through Plumtree there was more, through Plumtree and Hinson Creek, through that section more than any other place that I know of.

Spar is kind of a white, chalky-looking stuff, but it's hard, brittle. And they use it to make pottery out of. They had to go in and work it and drill holes in it and shoot it out. Then, when big hunks came out, you had to beat 'em up. Now something else has taken its place; same thing with mica.

Down here at Micaville, next to Burnsville, they do have a place there that operates on a small scale of mica yet.

Oh, mica, now, they used to use it for windows. You could get enough light through it to see. Why, you could get out a block twelve by fifteen inches, and it'd bring you a lot of money. Several thousand dollars. It sure was valuable.

A lot of it was scrappy, so they would have to sift it. They'd get the mica out of it and let the gravel go back into a pile.

Doyle I. Oakes, Sr., 1909 Avery County

Feldspar

For many years feldspar was our main mining, and many people around Micaville worked at that. Some mining is done there yet. Now, feldspar is found all through these mountain regions. You might find a vein, and this vein will carry you on several feet.

Now, vermiculite is mined on Green Mountain Road. They make dishes out of that, and sometimes it is used in guns and airplanes. For this, they just dig down, and they go from one mountain to another as long as the veins last.

One time in Micaville—now, this is feldspar—three men went in too soon, and the blast went off while they were in there. Course, it killed them.

Pearl Randolph, 1912 Yancey County

Peeling Tanbark

In the spring, we'd peel tanbark. We'd cut the trees down and peel the bark off of them. Cut it all up around 'em, you know, and dry it. It wasn't so awfully hard to peel 'em. It would slip off at the right time, early in the spring. Tanbark trees, we called 'em. Just chestnut oak.

Stack the bark up around, you know. Then we'd pull it off of the top of the mountain on brushes, down to where we could get it on a sled. Then we'd get it on a sled and bring it on down to where we could get it on a wagon. Then we'd take it on the wagon to Hayesville. Just me and the children.

Now, we just pulled that bark off of the tree, just like it was. We'd cut it, you know, all around, and then we had things to slip under it and prize it. Just prize it off. And they used that for tanning leather. We'd cut the tree down and get every bit of bark off of it that we could. The most we ever got for it was thirteen dollars a cord. And now it's about fifty or sixty dollars a cord.

Now, we did that in the spring. In May was the best time. It would peel easier in May than in any other time. That was the time the sap got just right.

Law, I don't know how many cords we'd get in a springtime! We got off all we could. And we'd drive the wagon up onto where they weighed it, you know. I guess we'd get about one and a half cords to a wagonload. It'd take us about a week to get a wagonload and get it there.

That was a lot of hard work for me and those children to get it cut off and put on the brush and on the sled and the wagon and get it to town.

Then we'd peel the pulpwood, you know. And we just got four dollars a cord for that. That was a lot heavier, too. But money would go twice as far as it will now — or three times.

Iowa Patterson, 1881 Clay County

Saving Up for Taxes

And Dad's land —
he had sixty-seven acres of land —
the tax on it was six dollars.
And we had to go and peel cherry bark
and peel haw bark to get money
to pay the tax with.
We'd get about thirty cents a day,
each one of us.
About seven cents a pound.
Yeah, we'd kill the tree.
Cut 'em down
and peel all the bark off of 'em.
And the haw,
it was about four feet tall.
We'd cut it off and hew it off.
And that's the way we growed up.

Stanley Hicks, 1911 Watauga County

The Old-time Tanner

I was born down at the east end of Stone Mountain. Stayed there till I was not quite twelve years old. Come up then to Bull Head country. When I started to school, it was just a log house up on the side of the mountain, just one big room.

John Brooks, I believe, was the first teacher I ever went to.

My daddy was an old-time tanner. Well, people would kill beef or anything. Course, as far as that goes, if they died, they'd skin 'em and take the hide to him, and he'd tan it.

If it was light enough, he could make it into shoe leather, and if it was heavy, he could make it into harness leather. And then, he'd black it, make it black; or he'd tan it, give it a tan color.

He tanned it with bark. He had vats he'd tan it in. But first, he had to lime it and pick the hair off. Lime it, soak it in a big pool. Scrape that hair off. Then work all that lime off, soak it in water and work it.

Had big knives to scrape it with. If you didn't get all that lime out, it'd be hard, you know. Then it would soon break.

And then, if the leather was light enough, he'd make shoes. The people at that time could make shoes. There'd be a shoemaker somewhere. A lot of people could make shoes. He made shoes for us kids some of the time. Sometimes he'd have somebody else to make 'em.

Course he had knives that he'd shave that inside part off with. He'd make that smooth and the same thickness all the way through.

He'd tan for people who would bring a hide in there. Then, if they wanted it all, he'd tan for so much a pound; or it they didn't want it all, he kept half of it. And then he would sell it to people who wanted it. Best I remember, it was about thirty cents a pound, is what he tanned it and sold it for.

Then when World War I come along, I had four brothers. Had three that went to France and one that went to camp. He would have went, but he took the flu, and the flu was so bad. I had four brothers in the army at one time.

That knocked me out of my education. They had to go off, and I was the only one helping at home, and I didn't get no education.

My daddy had four big vats. They was four feet square and eight feet long. Go down in the ground. Made out of white pine two inches thick. Had 'em fixed to hold water.

When the sap was up, they'd cut white oak trees, peel the bark off of them, and after it got dry, grind it to do this tanning with. Had a mill to grind it in.

Then he'd put that bark in the vats, you see, with the water. That's what he used to do the tanning with. Put the hide in there after they'd worked all the lime out of it and tanned it.

Had to leave the hide in them vats quite a while. He'd take it out about every day and kind of air it and put it back.

Then, after it was tanned, he'd finish it up with these knives that he had to shave with. Now, harness leather, he put oil on it, but shoe leather, he didn't put no oil on that.

Seems like he'd leave it in that lime for several days. But he'd take it out every day and air it. He had a reel set up over this long vat, and he'd start it on that and roll it on that reel for it to get air.

Then he'd put it back in there. And he'd take a hoe and start scraping till that hair started to slip off, and when it did, well, he was ready then to take them knives and scrape it off.

Then he had to keep soaking it in this big pool and working it till he got all that lime out of there. Then he put it in to tan. And it stayed for several days.

Now, if someone liked light-colored leather, he'd tan that with white oak bark. And, if they didn't, why, he'd tan it with the chestnut oak, and that was a dark color. It was red looking.

When he took it out, he'd put it on a beam, running down, and take one of them long knives and shave it down. He'd get all that rough part off inside, you see, and that's what made it smooth.

Josh Spicer, 1902 Alleghany County

Tanning Groundhog Hides

You just take the groundhog hide, skin it. Skin it out! Then take a bucket, pot, or anything and put you about a pint or a pint and a half of ashes, ashes out of a stove, fireplace, anything.

Put it down in there, put your hide in there, stir it up good and leave it overnight, and it'll take the hair off of it. Yeah, you put water in it enough to cover it up. Then the lye comes up, you see, and takes the hair off. Then you can take a knife or anything, you see, and scrape it all off clean.

Then get you some soap and be certain that you wash all the lye out of it before you tack it up. Then just stretch it out like I've got them on that board out there and tack it up.

Now, if you don't use soap and get the lye out of it, when you get ready to stretch it, it'll just pull apart. The lye would eat it up. You'll have to get it out before it eats it up. Just let it soak overnight.

See, that's what Dad made our shoestrings out of. You can work that and tan it and make shoe strings out of it. Now, to tan it, you just have to take it and rub it over your leg or a chair back or anything until you get it pliant. No, you can't tear it; ain't no way. I've got some strings downstairs in a pair of shoes that I fixed that way that, gosh, you can't never wear 'em out. No, you'll never wear 'em out! And you can take squirrel hides and make little strings to sew your shoes up with.

Stanley Hicks, 1911 Watauga County

The Poor Man's Mill

Now, when I was just a little fellow, I went to a poor man's mill, where you ground corn and pancake buckwheat, where you put the buckwheat in a little bowl and turned a little crank. Now, the poor man's mill run on a little stream of water. Down under the mountain, now, was the biggest creek up from the river, the Watauga River. Spice Creek Branch, they call it down here, was the one I went to as a little boy, nearly dying in snowstorms.

And they just had a little pond, and in dry weather like it is right now, you'd have to wait till they caught a pond of water to grind about a half a bushel.

Sometimes, Les and his wife would grind. He had it rigged up with a big handle up in the mill to pull the water gate on and off, up above the pond. The "water gate," they called it, with a spout that run into the water wheel. And his wife didn't know how much to pull it, and she'd be grinding for me and my younger brother. Les would be gone. And she'd get too much water turned on, and that little old mill house and them pillars felt like it was going to walk off down the branch!

They had a "toll dish," they called it, made out of wood. And they took two scoops out of a bushel and one out of a half; and I believe it held about a quart. Then, as times built up, prices built up, got higher. A-rolling it got higher. Some would build a new toll dish, but others just tacked a rim around the box—the toll dish—to make it about that much higher to take that much more corn. And that's the way you paid for getting your grinding done. That's how they lived, why they worked to put a mill up.

Ray Hicks, 1922 Watauga County

A Hatful of Corn

I've had to go sharpen the grist mill, you know. Get about a dollar, a dollar and a half. Take us about two or three days. See, I'd have to grind that and stay there all day for the toll.

When I'd sharpen it, I'd take a mill peck. That's a rock, and you just peck furrows in it, in the millstone. The stone was about forty inches across. I had to peck those furrows in it so it would grind.

When it would get warped, it wouldn't grind. It would just mash the corn and stuff up. When you see these millstones now and they are just smooth, that's where they're just wore out.

Now, these old millstones, it takes a certain grit of rock to make 'em. Takes a gray rock with this here flint in it. You can't just make 'em out of anything. You go in there, and it takes you about a week, two weeks to cut one out. You go back up in these hollows where these rocks is, and you just have to find it. You have to find the thickness you want.

These old people knowed where to go get 'em. You've got to get 'em with flint in 'em. If you don't, they wear out quick. And then you start these furrows. You cut 'em a little into where the eye is at; then you cut 'em wider, you know. Where the corn goes down through it, it's narrow there, and it gets wider all the time. So I'd help cut them out.

My grandpa,
he said he worked to raise his family
for a hatful of corn a day.
My grandpa worked at the mill,
and the miller would give him
a hatful of corn—
these old high hats, you know—
to work for him that day.
And he said
he had to pay his toll
out of that.
So when he got home,

he just barely had enough
to feed his young'uns one mess.

There was one old miller,
they said he would take all the corn
for the toll
and then swear to the sack.
Well, you see,
he just took it all.
You didn't get back home with nothing.
And Grandpa told his young'uns,
he said,
"If I live another year,
I'll never buy another grain of corn."

Stanley Hicks, 1911 Watauga County

Chapter 5. Of Religion

The rigorous, stark realities of mountain life demanded strong spiritual sustenance. There were times when a person's faith was all he had to hang on to. On Sunday mornings, the people of the hills climbed into the same wagons that they had used for farm work during the weekdays and headed over the ridges to church. Many times, with starched white apron and black bonnet, Mother would ride beside Papa in a straight chair while the children sat on the wagon floor on a quilt or "counterpin" to protect their Sunday clothes.

The preacher was the revered and respected leader of the community. Old-time hymns resonated against the rafters, and sermons bristled with vivid admonitions that prodded the consciences of the mountain people and sustained their faith through periods of illness or grief.

The Family Bible

I don't know
of a family
nowhere
that
didn't have a Bible.

And they believed what it said!

I still do!

Tom Pruitt, 1904 Alleghany County

Going to Church

Oh,
we went to church and had revivals
three weeks at a time.
And the preachers told it loud!
And they had a pretty good shouting time.
Lord, you never would miss a night.
You'd think the Devil would get you
that night!
And feed that preacher, law!
Hot biscuits,
ham!
Yeah, boys,
they'd preach it off!
Now, they'd tell it, wouldn't they?

If they could frighten 'em,
they'd frighten 'em.
Why, they'd just open Hell's door
and see the fire!
And *smell* it!
Yes, boy,
they'd tell it.
Service would go on for an hour
or an hour and a half.
Some singing
while they's a-having the altar call.

We had a Methodist church and a Baptist church.
We went to both of 'em.
What's the difference?
And the big meetings
would be in the fall.

Now,
a woman could never preach in church.
That was the worst thing.
Now, she might get up and speak
a few words
of how the Lord had blessed her.

A testimony.
You see,
the Bible says not to let the women preach.
The husband was the head of the house,
and it wasn't right
for the women to preach.
Now,
a woman could teach in Sunday school.
My mother taught for years and years.

Nannie Smith, 1888 Clay County

The Call to Preach

I want to tell you something important. You know, back in them days the souls of the children was a lot more precious than the education of the head.

They started a revival meetin' at Pleasant Grove Church. We had a schoolhouse right there in about three, four, or five hundred yards of where I was raised.

Went to school there as long as I went to school. And those ministers sent word out there they wanted to come out there to the schoolhouse where we was, to dismiss the school.

Run a meetin' there for a week. I made a profession right there in the school house where I got all my education and joined the church and was baptized.

There was forty-three of us baptized
that time.
Ice floatin',
the river full of ice then.
My younger sister and I
was baptized together.
They just waded us right out
into that river.
That was in February,
and ice was floatin' down that river.
One boy got his hand cut
on some of it,
but it didn't hurt.
The water was cold.

Actually,
you might think
that this was a fairy tale,
but I never got cold.

Later on, before them old ministers quit runnin' those meetings them days, I think they would be right close to their home. And those meetings met there at Landmark and right over here at Glade Creek Church. Run two weeks there and on over to Saddle Mountain. I don't know how many weeks they was. That batch was added to the number that belonged to Landmark.

Well, when I was twenty-seven years old, I begin to feel that, knowing that my spirit, my heart was going to preach. Well, for twenty-two months I fought it like a tiger. I didn't have a notion. I just figured that this was one time what the Lord wants, I wasn't going to do.

But I found out he was stronger than I was. That's one reason why I have some of my afflictions today. For that.

At last, when I did submit and finally started and was licensed in 1936, ordained in 1938, all my troubles were ended.

Well, I determined before that if I ever made one [a preacher], that if the Lord would help me and stand by me, that I would never yield to no man, regardless of what he preached. And I've kept that determination pretty good, if I do have to say so myself.

I believe this much with all my heart; fact of the matter, I know it: if God wants a man to preach, he's plenty able to give him something to say!

And if a man ain't got enough faith in God to trust him to give him something to say, the best thing to do is stay out of the pulpit. Because now, after going through all these battles of life that I went through, bein' blessed as many times as I have, I want you to plainly understand I've not been blessed to preach the gospel every time I've risen before the congregation.

You can feel the inspiration when it comes. Yes, you can. You can feel it and not only that, but the congregation feels it. But, if that congregation's sitting out there and don't care whether to eat or to starve, the Lord isn't gonna cram it down their throats.

He just don't work like that. That's the reason why, I think sometimes, that the individual minister is not to blame for being let down. The Lord shows those people, or tries to, at least, that unless they are humble in spirit, humble in heart, and are willing to accept his word and his spirit, he's not going to give it to 'em, nor to me, nor to no man.

And I count it just as much glory to God, for that matter, when I make a failure as I do when he, that spirit, gives me the revelation that I

can see these things to tell the children. It is. It's just as much glory to
him because that if they'd look at it like that, it proves to 'em that it's
not me.
    And I can't do it within myself.
    That's the point.
    And it, also,
    furthermore than that,
    it proves to 'em
    that when that spirit
    is a-dwelling' with my spirit,
    and my spirit
    is dwellin' with their spirits,
    then we're all one,
    together,
    and not divided in mind.
    And, well, that's what it takes!
When that spirit come, it's a reviving spirit. It's something that
revives you up, something that gives you something to strengthen your
faith and your hope, that you can hold on to till the next time.

I've made my failures as well as everybody else, of gettin' cold. That's
good for a man. Even though it's not exactly what he'd like to have, it's
still good for him. There ain't nothing in him but a man to start with.
    I lived in what they called the Depression. I come through that, and
I'm still alive. Back then, people was humble; they loved one another.
And they reverenced God more so than anything else.
    But just as soon as we come out of the Depression, and prosperity got
started, it started taking the humble spirit away from the people. And
it's got worse and worse and worse. I guess it'll go right on, unless
somethin' else hits 'em again.
    I've been in a lot of revival meetings personally myself. I have run
onto thirty-six sessions, hands going. Well, I've had some very joyous
times, and I've had times of sorrow. I was in a revival meetin' when my
mother died.
    When they came to association meetings, people rode their horses.
They come in buggies and wagons and what have ye. And in them days
we didn't take lunch out, either, to spread on the ground. At the end of
the session somebody went home with everybody else. They just took
'em home with 'em.
    I've slept on the floor, personally, myself, and at a stranger's house,
for that matter. That's what I was speaking of, that humble spirit....
Now anyone wouldn't think about that.

Fact of the matter—personally, right here I've had six piled on this floor right here myself and the beds full besides. I enjoyed it. They did, too, I reckon.

See, we have Friday and Saturday and Sunday. The associational works goes on Friday and Saturday. Nothing but preachin' on Sunday.

Anymore, though, they always spread dinner out on the ground or the table or like that. I'm not just as crazy over that as a lot of people is to start with. I still think we ought to take 'em home with us and let 'em eat.

I don't have any kind of musical instrument in my church. I don't think they have any business in there. I start the singing with my voice. I start 'em off, and they just fall in with me.

But we've got away from lining the songs out. We got away from that a whole lot because the older ones has died out, and the younger ones can't do it.

Used to, when a minister opened the service, before the prayer, he'd line out one of those old hymns, and they would sing it. But now we don't have anyone—fact of the matter, I'm the only one that can lead a song that belongs over here.

Only one thing to do, you gotta buckle in on it! That's all there is to it. I'm not a-braggin' about it, but I've got a bunch of children over there that would really fall in and help me. There ain't no question about that. When I get started, they'll start to help me out every bit they can. Not only that, but they're willing. There's a sister or two over there, too, that can lead some of the songs.

Personally, now, I like songs that's got all the parts to 'em, and everybody in there getting their part. You take those old time hymns. I don't know whether any of you ever heard them oldtimers get ahold of them or not.

Of course, everybody tried to sing, and that's what I like. If you was to come in over here to the church, we'd give you a book and expect you to use it.

I don't go for this choir business; now, half a dozen sittin' up over here doing the singing and everybody else sittin' back and looking on.

Get in there and do somethin' and then you might get somethin' out of it. I think anybody gets out of the service just about what they put in to start with. If you don't put nothin' in it, you certainly couldn't expect to get nothin' out of it.

If you was to open up your pocketbook, and it was empty; and if you never did put nothin' else in it, you never would get nothin' else out of it. That's all there is to it.

No, ma'am, I don't work on my sermons during the week. I don't go up there with nary bit in the world. I have raised before the congregation with my mind just as blank as that hole in that door yonder, as far as that's concerned.

I been blessed, I guess, when the Spirit was good, and I have thought that was just about the best way a man could rise, not to have nothing. Not to be able to meditate over it one bit in the world. Then you know you've got to depend on the Lord.

I certainly ain't gonna inject my ideas about the matter. Now, anybody can get up and say a few words and sit down there, but as far as preachin' the gospel, the gospel's the power of God unto salvation to he that believeth!

And if they ain't no power there, I don't care how much Bible I might quote, there's no gospel to it because the Spirit is not a-bearin' witness. And if the Spirit bears witness, then the gospel's gonna be preached outa me or whoever it might be. And I believe it's said, "How can they hear without a preacher, and how can ye preach except it be sent?"

Also, "Blessed are the feet of those that preach the gospel."

Millard F. Pruitt, 1911 Alleghany County

The Burden of My Conscience

Now, the old teachings back in the old churches, the organization that we had in these mountains when I was small, was the Primitive Baptist. They'd sing them there old mountain harmony songs.

And then today, why we ain't got no people like we used to have. They have their churches, but they don't live like they did back then, to have God's will. God is not dead; he's still like he was.

But you take them people back then—now, I know, I've seen them. There's a lot of people that won't believe it, probably, but you take people who's singing for a lot of show, with tenor and alto and bass, now, God ain't with you if your mind is like that. You've got to sing with God, the same as if you didn't know them other people was sitting there.

And when these people sung a song; there was one singing a song at one place and one at another. And just each one would sing until he got through the song: one would be done; another, halfway; and another, starting. And sing, take thirty minutes, maybe, to get one song finished.

They was a-singing to the praises of the Lord, not man. That's why God was with them.

And then they had their footwashing. The song that they sung was "Sinner in the church, church him, turn him out, and let the church roll on." Well, that's what happens today. They just keep him in there. There are so many bad, if they turned 'em out, they'd all be gone.

The footwashing. Now, they all come, and the women washed the women's feet; the men washed the men's in the love of Christ, of God. Not a-washing because they was dirty. You was supposed to have your feet clean when you went. All the Christians in the church, all the men Christians washed one another's feet, and the women washed the women's feet. And so it went on, and a lot of 'em in the country got to saying, "If you're going to have a footwashing, have it"; and they got to going with theirn dirty. And it busted it up, kindly.

But during the service, God give the words to them, each service, to say. And the preachers, they didn't read ahead or nothing. And, boy, them words would pour out when that Spirit would get him.

"Oh, God . . . ," I can hear that. They would just roll out. He would just read a text from the Bible. Couldn't read much, you know. A lot of 'em just learned to read out of the Bible. Never went to school. Said God would teach 'em. Said God said if you asked for wisdom, he'd give it to you if you were in the right way. And they just knowed how to read a little bit.

He'd just read that little bit of the text of the Bible and start, and he could preach an hour—or two hours. They usually preached two hours back then. Got on up then, and they said it wore the patience of the people out. And now they've cut it down to about thirty minutes.

Now, during that two hours there was so much Spirit that nobody went to sleep. When you see anybody go to sleep in a church, the Spirit's weak in that church. It's weak; ain't much there, as the old preacher said. Now, there was a Baptist church in a wood house, just a common old wood house when I was young, about sixteen or seventeen years old.

There was a old preacher, a bishop, living yet, getting up in years, seventy or eighty years old. And he was just as young. Said God had kept him for a purpose. And he was just as young and catty as a young man. So he started a revival, started a revival there. Sang. Preached. And I went. I liked to hear him, always liked to hear him from a young boy up.

Some of 'em would say, "I believe I was born saved." And the others would say that didn't do them no good, just as well to read a catalog to 'em as the Bible. Said they didn't get nothing out of it.

But I could really enjoy hearing 'em sing and preach. And so he preached that night, tried to, worked his shoulders, hit the pulpit with his fist. Now, they hit hard, come down, jarred!

When he got done, he just said, "I've got to quit. It ain't nothing here. Now, Christians," he said, "I don't know no names. I can't call no names of who's done against God." He said, "You people, Christians in here, go home tonight and fix this up with one another. You'uns got a grievance against one another, some way or another. Unless you'uns makes it up, I'll have to quit this revival. Ain't no spirit here. It's nothing. It might be a little speck of what they call 'lukewarm.'" He said, "I can't get my words; God won't give me no words to preach."

Well, I come back the next trip, about the middle of the revival, and they'd made 'er up and had it a-going. Straightened it out.

And so there was another man down yonder under the mountain where there was a bunch of these rough, young men drinking this here mountain moonshine whiskey. They was rough. They would rob you and kill you down in there of a night. So this preacher went down there and started a revival. And they throwed a rock through the window and broke it out. Fell in front of the pulpit. And they got out after him, the deacons did, with some others to help. And they run 'em in the woods around the church. They got so rough, they run 'em all off.

So there come another preacher. And so he went to preaching, and in there came another rock through the window, fell in front of the pulpit. They started out after him, and the preacher said, "Now, hold it, hold it! I'm a-running this revival. Hold it!" He just started preaching on and didn't get after 'em or nothing. And, before the revival was over, he had some of 'em in there and their souls saved.

'Cause they was a-running 'em was what was making 'em do it. But he just said, "let me preach on, even if they break every window out." And he just kept a-preaching. And they throwed one more rock, and that a smaller one. That ended it. At the last revival, some of them young men come in at the morning bell, come up, and got saved.

Some of the old Methodist preachers, and the Primitive Baptists, too, would ride horses and fix 'em a grove. They'd tack 'em a board up on a stump for a pulpit and preach in the summertime when it was pretty weather and have 'sociations outside. They didn't have no shelter. They would just preach every Sunday.

Now, that 'sociation was when all the Prims met up. Come out of Wilkes County and Alleghany. They come in over here and got started. Built that little church. All them preachers would come, and they would have a meeting sometimes for a month. 'Sociation, they called it.

Set dinner. And sing. And preach. And, all them preachers, it took a long time to get 'em all through.

"Amazing Grace" was one they sang [sings]. Now, when I go to singing that, it hits me! Now, that was the Spirit! Now, another song was one they called a "self pity" song. But you know, the Bible tells us to come humble. That's what it means.

[sings]
I'm just a-going over Jordan,
I'm just a-going over home.
I know dark clouds will gather o'er me,
And I know my pathway's rough and steep.

[speaks]
Now, if you live for God, your pathway is rough and steep.

[sings]
I know my pathway's rough and steep.
A golden field lays out before me,
While no more this heart shall beat.
I'm just a-going over Jordan,
I'm just a-going over home.
I'm going there to see my mother.
She said she'd shake my hand when I come.
I'm just a-going over Jordan.
I'm just a-going over home.

Now, that's just wonderful, sung. It's got a lot of meaning.

If that don't hit you, you ain't got nothing but the worldly spirit. That's all you got. The evil spirit. Now, songs like that won't cheer up anybody that's just got evil spirit in their heart. But say, if it's just partly evil, it'll kick 'em up enough till it'll come on out. And the heart will get, to say, pure.

We can't get perfect. We can't live perfect with the flesh. Now, what shows if you've got something, is when you do something wrong, it chastises you back.

Now, I've been with people, and I can tell what they've got. If it's drinking, it's drinking. That don't hurt 'em, fer as the Spirit, to take a drink. That just brings the good out of you, if it's in there. But the alcohol just brings out the good or the bad, if it's in there.

But I could tell, after I worked with 'em for a while, how they was.

They'd come around me, and they'd say, "Ray, you've got something that's coming in us, that we want to be around you. They's something in you that makes us feel good. What is it?"

I said, "That's that there, that's in me, that I wouldn't do you a wrong if I knowed it with my mind." And I said, "Or I'd just do it unthoughty if I did. And think of it afterwards and punish for it." Now, I've done that. Do wrong before I thought, unthoughted, then punish for it. Six months before I'd get it off of me, a burden of my conscience.

Another thing, now, when you're young in God—now, God don't work with the old ones; God don't deal with old people like he does with the young. It carries out his life, a-raising of the children back, in the seed of life. After the seed leaves, you can go back, like the Bible says, "Once to man, and twice to child." God don't deal with you no more strong, like he did when you was in your teens, raising the seed of the people.

God is a-talking to every individual, through your ears here. One side will say—the evil spirit will say—"Yeah, do that; it's all right." It'll talk, it'll talk to you a hundred times faster than the other. It'll go a hundred words to fifty of the good.

The good is slow. It don't talk fast to you like the evil. It'll say, "Yes, you'll make it." And that there Spirit, boys, in your ear, I've had it to call me there. It'll say, "Ray," and that was a smooth sound; it'll say, "Stick to me. That other'll lead you astray."

If I'd a-listened to that evil spirit when I come up in this mountain here, a-drinking with the evil men, I wouldn't a-been living; I could have been killed years ago like a lot of others got killed. The Bible says, you know, "Go with a bunch. But hunt your bunch to go with." And them's hard to find when you's like I was. There's not many you can find to go with. That's why I had to go by myself.

> And out in the woods, now,
> gathering herbs,
> that's where I could get the closest to God.
> I'd get on them mountains.
> I mean after I come on in that.
> Now, back at one time,
> I was scared in the woods —
> of the canyons and the big rock cliffs and caves.
> I was scared of bears and all that.
> And I kept shunning them rocks.
> Feel bad to get under the shelter of them.

So finally, I was in the woods and got to studying,
a-looking at God's creation.
What a wonderful, powerful God he is!
Of all the herbs I was a-gathering,
with all the little veins in the leaves,
the sap veins that goes to the roots,
the same as our body.
And the little ants, out there,
and the birds.

The little ant's out there
trying to make it a living,
cutting a log out.
It'll come out and drop it off.
And then there's a bird there
that God created to eat him if he could
for his food.
Now, God give that ant a protection
just like he give us.
And the bird,
he give the bird
to know to sound that wood with his beak.
Now, if it knowed just to keep quiet,
it could catch every ant it was,
that bird could.
But they was give to make a noise
so ants could survive to grow food.
And when that bill would rattle,
you couldn't see a ant nowhere.
They all run in there and squatted down,
just right still.
And then that bird will peck in and find them,
enough to make out with its food.
Course, they get hungry sometimes.

And a hornet will catch every fly there was,
that flies around the porch
or out in the woods.
They'll go around,
just zzzzzzzzzz — zzzzzzzzzz,
and they'll get 'em to feed their young.

But God fixed to make it hard
on everything that lives
so it can't get so big and easy with it.

And so there was the rocks
and all the cliffs and the timber.
You could see God in everything,
in all of it.
You know, it said,
"God is all in all."
And I got to where I could see God
in everything that goes on.
God's in it all, in the whole being.

But now, he give it
to make it look bad to us a lot of times
in our way of being depressed in things
with your loved ones a-passing away
and the rough things that comes on.
But now, he's a-ruling years ahead
to bring good.
Evil goes through there and brings good.
But you, through your whole lifetime,
it's a-hurting you;
but it's a-going on, coming good,
with the seed a-going on.
And that's where it says,
"God is all in all."
But right at the time,
like I said,
the people will think it's a bad age.
It is in our lifetime,
but it'll go on.
I've seen it in my life:
the good will go on and bring bad,
and the bad will bring good.
And it'll go on, side by side.

Ray Hicks, 1922 Watauga County

Mountain Philosophy

This fellow says, "I want you to tell me the difference between a white lie and a black lie."

I said, "Now, a white lie is when somebody has done a pretty bad thing. And instead of speaking up to make troubles worser, you just hint around and speak a few short words and cut it off to save trouble."

Well, the Bible says, "Blessed is the peacemaker." That means, if you know the truth, don't tell it and cause more trouble. Now, you can just hint around and give him enough to put him off. And hold it back.

Now, that's what they call a white lie.

And now, the black one, the black lie is when they told a big 'un on him, and hit not true! And three more to prop it up with!

Now, that's what the difference between a white lie and a black lie is.

And, see, they had always thought, they said, that a lie is just a lie!

And here's something else I can put in. If you steal in the daytime, it ain't as bad as stealing in the dark. And people would talk to me, and they'd say, "Ray, it ain't no difference."

It is! Now, that there man out there in the light—well, you go to somebody's house to steal something, he's got a chance to see you. But after night, you're in the dark. And the Bible says, "A man loves dark because his deeds is evil."

Well, a fellow who was out there stealing in the daytime, he ain't really a-stealing. He maybe was just up agin it in the olden time.

Now, maybe this other fellow had a right smart of corn in his crib, and he'd slip there and get a turn.

One fellow, now—listen to this. This is true. Now, this fellow had this corn, and it dried up. And he knowed this other fellow, if he went and asked him for a wagon load out of the crib, he wouldn't give it.

But he went there of a night and took a wagon load of his corn. Well, the next year he planted back, made a good yield. And he didn't slip it back. He went back and told him that he'd took a wagon load that fall when hisn was drying up.

And this fellow says, "If you took one wagon load and I didn't know it, you might have got two." Now, he took it back and went and told him.

He ought to have slipped it back!

Now, that's what caused a lot of the stealing back in the olden times. Cause a lot of them close people, who raised a lot of corn, watched it and kept it a year ahead, wouldn't let you have none if you went and asked for it! Said they might need it.

Well now, a lot had to steal to live! And that's why I said while ago that it works for good. God's the ruler.

Now, it ain't wrong to steal if you get to where you have to for food. If you got a little bunch of chaps, and you go and ask for it first.

Try several days. And if you can't find nobody that will let you have nothing, if you can get it and they don't know it, you ain't done no wrong. God is the ruler. He'll help you get it!

He'll watch over you. And then you go work it through somebody else. Pay it back!

It don't have to be the person you got it off of. They're all God's people. Just go on and give it to somebody that's a-punishin'.

If you see with your eyes little young'uns that's naked and sufferin', you don't have to give it to the one you took it off of. He's doing good! Go give it to one out here that ain't got nothin'. Little children that punishes, that don't know no better. Give it to them. Turn it back to them, and God will give you a reward.

Jesus said, "Blessed is the little children." The Saviour of the world was with the little children all the time, playing with them and loving them up.

He likes the old ones, but children is what he loves the most because they didn't know how, just like his birds, little birds.

> He'll always make a way
> to save the seed of everything,
> to help it to get food
> because that little bird is in the nest.
> It can't fly.
> It has to be teached by the old ones
> how to make a living,
> to watch for the fox,
> the snakes,
> the bird hawks.

And a lot of 'em, the mother gets killed just about the time I seed it. The mother gets killed, or something catches her. She dies. And these here birds in the nest just lacks just a little bit, enough to fly out of the nest. For several days she trains 'em when they get out of the nest.

And they get out there and don't know how to get around, and the snakes and all eats 'em all up.

But a lot of times God is there, and they'll make it, even if they do fall out of the nest. It's give to them, just the same way it's give to us.

> It was give to me.

That's the reason I believe it.
I believe it was give to me
when I was small.
I wasn't even three.
I had to do most of my own training.
And I'll tell anybody one thing:
when you get your own training
from the book in you,
from God and creation,
you've got something
besides reading it out of another book.
That's somebody else's teaching.
You've got it all.
And it stays.

Ray Hicks, 1922 Watauga County

The Funeral

When someone died, we'd wash 'em from head to foot. And set up. People come in and set up. And they [the deceased] would lay with their mouths open and their eyes plumb glared. Scare anybody that was scary.

Why, ain't you seen 'em or heard of 'em? Ain't I a-telling it right? Law! Now, I don't reckon the family ever had to fix the body. Some neighbors would come in.

The funeral was at the church, and maybe for one hour the preacher would tell, "Now, this feller's gone to heaven, and you'd better get ready to go!"

Ain't you never been there? And they'd just keep a-telling it and walking the floor. Now they think five minutes is a good, long time!

But back then the preacher would still be preaching, and night a-coming on. He'd just be walking the floor. "You're going to go home, and you're going to miss this mother." It'd be a mother, you know. And there all the children would sit. Hard? It was awful!

In the wintertime, with the ground frozen, it wasn't easy. They'd just have to wait till the ground thawed or something. It was bad. Just happened, maybe, that one had passed away while it was so bad. It would be just a day or two, usually, till they could dig the grave.

Nannie Smith, 1888 Clay County

Chapter 6. Medicines, Plants, and Herbs

Physical complaints were generally treated with a combination of trial and error, time-tested home remedies, common sense, and pure luck. In many cases, ills, both physical and mental, just cured themselves, since the hardy mountain people had little time to bemoan their weaknesses. With fresh air, plain country food, and plenty of outdoor exercise, they maintained a strong resistance. Mental and emotional ills, being looked upon with suspicion, were given little berth.

Almost every locality boasted its "Old Doctor So-and-So" stories, but the resolute mountaineer rarely presented himself as a patient unless he was desperate indeed. The deeply ingrained ethic of independence decreed that one not call on outside help except as a last resort.

In the meantime, Granny kept her store of herbs close at hand, ready to concoct teas and poultices for whatever the ailment might be.

Snakebite Remedy

This here feller, he would come down to the grocery store and trade, bring his herbs. And he told my dad, said he'd been snake-bit two or three times. On the face, he'd been bit, and he says, "Now, I carry a pint of whiskey, of the mountain-best whiskey that could ever be made, pure whiskey." He says, "I carry my whiskey when I go into that Stone Mountain and three bottles of turpentine."

The turpentine, at that time, was in a little flat bottle that didn't hold much. He said, "I carry three bottles of it, and when I get bit, I hold the first bottle to the wound, and," he says, "you can *see* the poison go out in it. Then throw it away. And then the second bottle, you can see a little poison go out in hit. Throw hit away; then hold the third 'un to it, and," said, "you couldn't see none go out in the turpentine. And," he said, "get it to it just as quick as you can, before it went in your bloodstream; then," said, "drink your whiskey and you's well."

And said, "Set down about thirty minutes and drink your whiskey. Don't walk." He said the whiskey, the alcohol, took care of what was left, till if it went through your bloodstream, it would just make you a little dizzy for about thirty minutes. Said not walk, right at the start.

And, another thing, now. What kills more people ain't the snakebite; it's fear! A-scared that they've got it, and their heart quits! I come near a-dying before I got to the house. Shock! There ain't enough poison to hurt you; your heart fails you.

Just say, "I've got it! I've got it!" Just up and say, "I've got it!" And just fear, like a rabbit does—you can take a rabbit, I mean a jackrabbit, they say. (I never did try.) They say you can hem a jackrabbit, and a lot of them'll just fall dead. Half of 'em or more, right in the field where they was hemmed, fall down and go to kicking and dying because they was hemmed up. Heart failed 'em, they say.

And that's the way they die with the snakebites, now. They die with fear before they can get to do anything. And then a-running can help, too, there. The poison, hit a-spreadin' through the bloodstream, a-runnin' and gettin' hot. Just take off a-running! Just out of their minds. Just excited, don't even know if they was to run against a tree or anything.

I've been with 'em that done that. They'd get hurt. Fall on a snag or rock, and I'd run and grab 'em, to save 'em, get their mind back. They would have run off a rock and killed theirself. They was heading out to get turpentine. If they'd just laid down, the snakebite might wouldn't have killed alot of 'em, with nothin' done. They'd a been plenty of 'em that would have lived.

A lot of 'em, now, would get bit, and they'd pack dirt, pack that black soil dirt on 'em, where they got bit. Yeah, they'd wet that dirt, or most of the time, it was already wet in this mountain. Just squeeze it up. Yeah, it'll draw poison out, that dirt will, that black soil with acid in it. You can get cut and put it on it, and it'll be well in three days with no medicine, if you heal good.

I'd fill that place full of dirt,
and they'd grab me and they'd say,
"Gosh, Ray,
that'll put infection in it till it'll kill you,
rubbing that poison dirt in it."
Now, you can't teach me that;
I've done went through it.
That dirt is clean!
Now, you might be thinking about dirt around the house.
All of your soil in the mountains
where the people don't stay—
well, God's creation is pure,

clean as your drinking water.
Perfect soil.
But now, where people stays,
and animals, and cattle, sheep, like that,
I wouldn't rub none on my finger,
unless I dug down pretty deep.
I wouldn't rub no topsoil on it.
But now, in the mountains
with that timber,
that sugar-tree soil, and ash.
Now, hemlock soil will ruin your cut,
to rub soil from under it.
Hemlock pine soil —
too much acid.
See, it's just full of acid.

Ray Hicks, 1922 Watauga County

Onion Poultice

People could treat their own illnesses.
My grandmother could treat anything.
She could treat you any way
for any kind of ailment
with roots, herbs, heat, or something.
Home remedies.
For croup,
she'd cook these onions.
Cook a big skillet of onions.
Make a poultice out of it
and lay it on your chest
to break the croup up.
See,
she'd take something like a flour sack
and sew it up.
Make a bag out of it.
Fill it full of hot onions.
I guess it was the heat that done it.
Onions held the heat, you know.
I guess that was the secret of it.

George Perkins, 1916 Mitchell County

Strange Concoctions

My earliest recollection of a doctor
was Dr. Heighway,
who lived right across the street.
He made his own pills.
And I can see him right now
with his case open,
dumping different, horrible things
in papers.

You didn't take them in capsules.
You took them in papers.
Folded them up.
Then you opened them up
and dumped them on your tongue
and swallowed water.

Sometimes you'd rather die than take it!

Emily Cooper Davidson, 1894 Cherokee County

Early Surgery

When our old doctor
first started out,
the first surgery they did
was on a table.
On a kitchen table
by lamplight.
That was appendicitis.
Oh, yes,
the patient survived.
That was Dr. Sloop.
He was certainly a wonderful doctor.

Winnie Biggerstaff, 1904 McDowell County

Infant Deaths

Ialways had a doctor with every one of my babies when they were born, but I never did go to a hospital. I never even went to be doctored. Just whenever it was time, we always sent for a doctor. And he always got there in time.

When someone died, they hauled 'em in a wagon. Just put 'em in a coffin—not a casket, now. A coffin is a different thing. It's just a wooden box, made bigger up across the shoulders. There was a man that made 'em and sold 'em. Now, they lined 'em inside and padded 'em with cotton. Put a pillow in. There was women that followed that, you know, and cut lace. Just take the cloth and cut lace. And you'd be surprised how pretty it would be, put on the pillow slip and around the edge of the coffin, where the ladies would bury their babies.

There was a lot of babies that died. That was hard on the mothers, but many of 'em died. A lot of 'em wasn't half took care of. They didn't have a way to take care of them like they should have been.

I lost one; my second baby died. It lacked three days of being four months old. A great big, fat baby boy. Bronchopneumonia. Just choked it to death.

The doctors could have saved it now. But doctors back then had to ride horses from Hayesville. And way up here, well, they couldn't get up here quick. You had to go after them. Had no way to call them.

In the wintertime, snow, storms. We had an old doctor; he come to my house when there'd be the awfullest storms a-going that you ever seen. But they didn't charge much. They didn't charge nothing like they do now. No, not nothing to talk about.

Iowa Patterson, 1881 Clay County

The Toothache

There wasn't any dentists here,
and I remember one time
I had the toothache,
and I went and got a watchmaker
to pull my tooth.

Had no numbing.
Just pulled it right out!
Yeah, it was painful,
but not near as painful
as that tooth a-stayin' in there!

We had the old wood heater.
And I'd laid down beside the wood heater
and tried to sleep for several nights,
and I'd blistered my whole jaw.
That was the only way
I could get any relief from it
was the heat from the heater.

So I got up that morning
and walked about four miles
and got the watchmaker to pull my tooth.
I'd heard he'd pull teeth.
I guess I was twelve or fourteen.

Ralph Crouse, 1922 Alleghany County

Blackgum Toothbrushes

Now, people didn't used to have toothbrushes
like we do now.
They just chewed their toothbrushes.
Just break a switch off of a blackgum tree
and just chew 'em.
It'd be just like a brush.
And you'd clean your teeth with that.

And they used soda.
Some people tried to take care of their teeth,
but hundreds of them neglected 'em.
And when a person got old,
they didn't have no teeth then.
There was no way to get 'em.
They didn't have no glasses that was worth anything.
When you was old,

you were just as old as you was,
and there was no helping it.

If you didn't have a hair on your head,
or if you didn't have a tooth in your mouth,
or if you couldn't see,
you weren't worth anything.
There was not a thing you could do about it.

Iowa Patterson, 1881 Clay County

No Barber Shops

Well,
it was just like cuttin' your hair.
They didn't have barber shops,
and only a few people would cut your hair.
Lot of times
on Sunday
if you wanted a haircut,
you'd go and stay at a neighbor's
and stay all day on Sunday
to get your hair cut.

And he didn't make no charge.
If you had a dime or a nickel
that you could spare,
why,
all right.
You'd give it to him.

And if you didn't have any money,
you just thanked him for it.

Ralph Crouse, 1922 Alleghany County

The Signs

Now,
they'd plant by the signs.
You'd plant what's above the ground;
you'd have to plant that
when the sign's in the head.
Course, now,
the cucumbers,
we planted them
when the sign's in the feet.
Because they run.
Anything like pumpkin,
squash, cucumber, and beans —
the runners —
you plant when the sign's in the feet.
Now,
there's some parts of the body
you'd better not plant in,
because it'll stink!
Well,
it won't do no good;
it's a barren sign.
If you plant in that sign,
you won't make nothing.

Tennie Cloer, 1886 Cherokee County

Pick-Breeches

My dad took me and my older sister and brother a-gatherin' herbs. And he stealed this here teaberry, which we called mountain tea. And birch oil, which they call it mahagony, anymore. Well, we called it black birch and white birch and silver birch. Now, they say that's silver birch, what we called black birch.

But, still, as I could study on it, in my life, as I come along, the chain of life, of the generations of people coming along all the time, the young a-coming along, and the old a-going out, it was just as good to call it black birch as silver birch. As long as each one knows what it means.

It just changes in the generations of people; it's just like everything's done now to change it, to make it hit again. You know, anything gets old, and you can change it and it makes it do better awhile. And then you change it back.

They changed Pick-Breeches to Mountain Dale. And what happened, why they changed it to Mountain Dale, the times changed, and it got to be a little bigger living. They thought that sounded a little better. Pick-Breeches was too hillbilly.

Now they've got a church built up in there. And back when they called it Pick-Breeches, it was wild up in there. Didn't have no church and no religious people hardly.

They said the way it got its name, Pick-Breeches, was them there, what they call in the Jack Tales, "bumberry briars." There was an old name, now, "bumberry." I wouldn't know what they call it anymore. They was bumberry briars up there, and they don't grow any blackberries. You can build a fence with 'em. It ain't nothing can get through 'em, that kind of briars. You can lay a lot together, and cattle or nothing won't try 'em. And they's a lot of 'em up in there.

And they come in a few people who had pretty good clothes; and the first women's stockings, the hose that they wore, if a briar picked 'em, they'd run. And just ruined 'em. And they got up in there and got them picked. And the stockings fell off of the women before they got back out, and they named it Pick-Breeches. And the men tore their breeches' legs open on snags and everything. And holly—it was holly up in there —and it had big thorns on the leaves. So they named it Pick-Breeches. Means you couldn't get out unless you got picked.

Then they got a church built, started, and it's going yet today. What is the organization of that branch? Baptist? It's Baptist. And that gave it the name for the new people who don't know no better, who growed up younger. Mountain Dale. And that's all they know it was named unless somebody like me can tell 'em.

Ray Hicks, 1922 Watauga County

Digging Ginseng

There was a lot of herbs that they used to buy here. Now, take sassafras bark and wild cherry bark. They'll still buy that.

And ginseng, goldenseal, red root or coon root, whatever you want to call it. Yellowroot, you can still sell those today.

Back when I was a boy, you could just carry it to the grocery store. If you had a pound of dried ginseng, see, you could get about twenty dollars, sixteen to twenty dollars for it. Now, it takes three pounds of green 'seng to make a pound of dried 'seng.

No, it's not hard to find. If you get in the mountain where you can find it, why, you might dig a pound of ginseng in thirty minutes.

It takes a plant a long time to grow. About eight to ten years to harvest it.

Just certain parts of the mountains. It's got to be rich dirt, but it'll grow most anywhere. But if it's cultivated, they won't pay you as much for it. It grows faster. Don't grow wild.

Now, the root is what you harvest of the ginseng, not the top. They don't want the top.

Back when I was growing up, why, you didn't dig ginseng until the berries got ripe, and you always sowed the berries back to keep it coming. But now it's very scarce.

Ralph Crouse, 1922 Alleghany County

A Hardy Generation

Back then, my grandmother and all of us would go into the mountains there and dig roots and herbs. Dig the roots of wild cherries. Dig these ginger roots. Bring 'em in and dry 'em. Bring 'em to Buladean down here, to the stores and trade 'em for sugar, coffee, whatever we needed. Stand-Back.

I don't know how long Stand-Back has been going. Back in the twenties, she'd buy a quarter's worth of Stand-Back. Seems like she'd get ten or twelve packs for a quarter. And we'd all take them when we had a headache.

My generation was an old generation. They lived to be up towards their hundreds, you know. One time, one of my aunts was down here trading roots and herbs, and one of these salesmen was down there talking. Trying to make a sale.

But he stepped back when she come in with her roots and herbs under her arm, on her hip. And she traded, went on, traded with the merchants there for whatever worldly goods she needed, you know.

The salesman was sitting there, looking around. And, really, he was just amazed at that old woman having roots and herbs to sell. Going into the mountain to pull 'em, dryin' 'em, bringin' 'em to sell.

Then she looked around and said, "Mammy will bring her roots in tomorrow. They wasn't hardly dry enough."

See, she was about seventy years old, and her mammy was about ninety. That was a fact! My granny lived to be a hundred and three. And she was strong.

Those people were hardy people. They're the only ones that lived, you know. The weaker died off. There was no medications much, or anything.

Now, they were a hardy generation, a working generation. Old generation. Outdoor work helped to harden them. They adapted themselves to the way they lived and eat. They eat the best of foods, I'd say. Nutritious foods.

When they come to adding all these things to flour, I'd say it started tearing part of your food values down. Probably adding things to your system that you didn't need.

George Perkins, 1916 Mitchell County

Chapter 7. Animals

It is doubtful that men could have conquered the mountain wilderness without the help of their animals. First with oxen and then mules they moved the huge timbers and broke the ground. Because of his strong dependence upon them, the western Carolinian usually treated his animals well. However, some work stock lived a harsh, cruel life.

Childhood memories vividly recall the days when Mama would pick the geese for the feather beds or the time of evening chores when a youngster would chase the cows up for milking.

Wild game was plentiful in the mountains, and the streams brimmed with fish, but a sense of wise conservation directed that one not take more than he actually needed.

Raising Geese

There was eleven children in our family, and five of us are still living.

I am Pearl Marshall, Pearl Franklin Marshall, daughter of Samuel Leroy Franklin. And we are the fifth generation down from Benjamin Franklin.

Our mother and father, they were among the very first settlers in what is called Montezuma now. It used to be called Bull Scrape!

They used to sort cattle here, and the bulls would fight. So they called it Bull Scrape. Well, later on, a few years later when it got more settled, an Indian passed through. His name was Montezuma, and they named this place Montezuma after that Indian that passed through here.

Now, our father and mother lived about a half a mile from the center of Montezuma down the Pineola Road, and it was called Goose Hollow.

See,
our mother raised geese,
and she had a goose
that lived to be sixty-five years old.

The way she could remember
the age of it,
she had a son
born the same spring as the goose.

Well,
we picked the feathers off the geese
and made feather beds.
Slept on feather beds
and feather pillows.
Still have 'em.
My mother made feather beds
for each one of the children.

And you know that old Pied
that lived so long?
That old Pied goose?
She was named Pied,
that old goose.

When feather-picking time come,
my mother would say,
"It's time to pick the geese."
Old Pied, when she heard that,
she was gone!
She hid,
and she never got picked!
Those old geese never liked
to have their feathers picked.
My mother would spread a sack
over her lap,
and she'd have a pouch
over to the right
to put their feathers in.
She'd stick their heads
back under her arm
and get their tail and their feet
in this hand,
and then she began
to pick those geese.

You didn't pull the down out;

you just pulled the top feathers.
They'd squall,
and they'd bite you, too,
if you let their head get out
from under your arm!

The old ganders,
they were mean!
They would grab you by the leg
and beat you with the butt
of their wings
if they could get a hold of you.

The gander, you know,
was the male;
and the goose was the female.
And that old gander,
he'd flip his head
and take out after you!
Now,
he knew better
than to mess with the older ones,
but he used to get after me,
that old gander with his long legs.
And I'd let him get up so close to me,
and I'd get him by the neck
and hold him up.
Then,
when I let him loose,
he'd leave me!

I'll tell you one thing:
they were very good for protection
because if anyone came in there
that they didn't think belonged there,
they made such a noise!
People would get afraid of them.
They were afraid of the ganders!
They would have come in the house
if they could have,
but we kept a fence around the yard.

Mrs. Pearl Marshall, 1904
Mrs. Hettie Loven, 1899 (sisters) Avery County

Balky Oxen

People in this county have always been hard-working people, them that would work. Some of 'em, you know, are kindly on the lazy side, but the biggest part of 'em actually do work.

The highway went down here from Newland to Elk Park. I worked on that back when I was about sixteen years old. My father was from this area, and my grandfather was from this area. My father did carpentry work, and he was pretty good at that. My dad was born in 1884.

My dad remembers down in Little Elk, below Elk Park, when they used to haul lumber out on a sled with a team of oxen. The winter was so hard back then, it [snow] would drift over the top of the fences and would pack so hard that instead of going around the curves, they'd go straight over the snow.

His oxen, sometimes, would get balky and didn't want to pull, and he'd take some of their feed and put up in front of them and make 'em come to it. Then he'd go up a little farther and make them come to it again. Over a grade. Then after they got over the grade, they was okay.

Now, you had to know pretty well about oxen, how to work 'em, or they was awful balky. If you didn't know how to maneuver 'em, they'd get the best of you. They would do what they wanted to.

As a rule, oxen won't get violent. Because, you see, they was bulls, and they have been castrated and made steers out of 'em. Which, you see, they are gentle then. They have worked bulls, but now, they can get mean!

Now, I went down to my granddad's place to help a fellow from Avery County who had some steers down there and some bulls, and he wanted 'em de-horned. And he wanted to castrate some of the bulls. So me and this other fellow, we went out to bring 'em in, and there was one bull that tried to attack him.

So he picked him up a big rock and struck him in the side of the head, and the bull sank to his knees. So we went up to him and went to whipping him with a switch, and he went on in for us.

He seen we had the best of him. So we took him on in the barn, tied him up, and went ahead and did what we had to do. De-horned him and everything. Then there was several more of them that didn't do us thataway. They went on in very calm.

Doyle I. Oakes, Sr., 1909 Avery County

Giving the Mules a Rest

We,
at home,
always had a team.
We had to have a team to work.
So far as going out of a Sunday,
we generally had a mule to ride.

But sometimes,
when we'd plow them mules all week,
we'd let them rest of a Sunday
because they was tired.
And we'd take it a-foot,
you know.

Henley Crawford, 1879 Clay County

Our Pride and Joy

When I was little, we had horses, dogs. Everybody had his own horse. We rode horseback. Oh, yes. I had a horse of my own.

I could ride from the time my dad could get me on a horse behind him. I don't remember learning to ride, I was so little. Sometimes he would take me up in front. And then I had a horse of my own.

I had a sidesaddle. But later, I had the other saddle. I remember the first divided skirts. We thought they were going to be terrible. We had riding suits. They came down halfway below your knees. And mine was made out of a brown denim. To be washed.

Everywhere you went, you rode horseback. If you wanted to go to Murphy, you went horseback. I'd go alone, by myself.

And we hitched our horses where Parker's Drug store is now. There were big elm trees. And there were hitching posts, they called 'em. Well, planks from one tree to another one. And there were places there you could hitch your horse. Go on and leave him. Just like parking your car.

There was a watering trough in east Murphy. We always went by and watered our horse. Before that, there was a creek that we always went through, and the horse always stopped and got a drink out of this creek.

When the road was changed, when they built better roads, they built a watering trough so the horses could get water. They had to think about their horses. Oh, yes, most people were good to their horses.

But some people were not kind to their horses. They were not well fed. Some people didn't feed them like they should, or shelter them. But our horses were prized. Our pride and joy.

Kate Hayes, 1892 Cherokee County

No Stock Law

There was no stock law.
The people fenced in their crops,
and the animals ran loose,
you know.
Even here in Murphy,
I've heard about cows in the streets.
In those days
there were many, many chestnut trees,
and the hogs would go into the mountains
and get real fat on the chestnuts.
And they all had to be marked
in their ears
so people would know their own stock,
you see.
I remember
when they would take a lot of food
and go to the mountains
to look for their stock,
and they'd bring them back
in the fall.
And I remember
when the law changed
so that
they would have a stock law.

Thelma Penland Axley, 1906 Clay County

Breaking a Cow That Kicked

Had an old Jersey cow
a man couldn't milk.
Tied her to the fence out there.
Had a stub tail.
Tied it to the fence.
Head, too.
And she'd kick!
Hurt me bad.
I's a-usin' a fence rail on her,
to tell the truth about it.
I's a-usin' it, too!
I wasn't playin' with her.
After that I could milk all day
out there anywhere,
and she wouldn't move.
One old lady came by,
and she called over here,
"That boy got to where he can milk yet?"
Dad said,
"He's too darn mean to tell.
He's been a-beatin' the cow
with a fence rail!"

Tom Pruitt, 1904 Alleghany County

Just Like People

Now, some horses and cattle, to milk 'em, you've got to get rough with 'em, just make out like you're rough with your voice, or show 'em that you're boss. Well, now you hit another 'un, if you talk ill to her or grumble or hit 'er or anything, she won't give 'er milk down. You've got to talk good to her and sing to her.

Sing a song. They'll turn their head and listen. Well, you could just sing any kind of song you would sing, just an old song like we'd sing in the mountains. But they usually, now, the animals, to go back, that kind is just like people.

Now one—it had to be like that—they liked religious songs. And one you had to handle rough, like the hillbilly songs. But the one that was humble there—her nerves, just like people—you'd have to sing a religious song to 'er.

And they'd stand, and I'd milk with both hands. Up there to the milk gap, I'd sing to my cows; I'd milk three or four. I had to milk 'em all the time.

Ray Hicks, 1922 Watauga County

The Mast

Now,
back in those days,
we never knowed what it was
to miss a big mast.
The mountains was full back in those days,
and you never knowed a thing about missing 'em.
Mast,
that's acorns and chestnuts and things
that grow on the trees,
that falls,
that the hogs eat.

Well, we always had a big bunch of hogs, and we'd go out there about November and gather 'em up and drive 'em in.

And they'd be so fat they couldn't walk, some of 'em.

See, we'd gather 'em up in the spring, take a day's drive, and put 'em in them big mountains. Well, the acorns that fell the fall before, what we called the big oak acorns, was still on the ground and a-sproutin'. Well, it was just like driving them hogs into a corn crib.

Well, they lived on them till the mast fell that fall. And so it began the next fall, you see.

Then, when we wanted to bring the hogs back home, we'd go out there and round them up and drive 'em back. No, we didn't have too much trouble finding them. They were there where they had plenty to eat. And they'd generally range in a certain boundary. They wouldn't get off too far, hardly ever.

Everybody had a mark.
And everybody,

neighbors around,
knowed one another's marks.
Ours was a swallow fork in the left
and a overslope in the right.
Ears, that is!
Just take the ear and give it a top slope.
Yeah!
Took the top out of each ear.

A swallow fork in the left.
We'd just take up the ear
and take a big piece out
of the middle of it.
Cut it way down in its ear.
And when they come up,
their ears was sore for it!

Well,
we generally always done that
when they was pigs,
you know.
We didn't wait till they got to be big hogs
to mark 'em.
We'd do it when they was young,
you know.
One man would just pick 'em up
and hold 'em,
and we'd mark 'em.

Oh,
they'd squeal a little,
but it was soon over with.

Henley Crawford, 1879 Clay County

Losing the Cud

The rhododendron, they call it now, we used to call it "laurel"; and the other, they call it "laurel" now, we called it "ivy." It's poison; it'd kill sheep, cattle. They'll eat it in the wintertime when they're snowed up.

The laurel, the "rhododendron," now they call it, won't poison 'em, but it'll just starve 'em to death. It'll just cause 'em to vomit all their eating up all the time. But what we called "ivy," what they call "laurel" now, it'd kill 'em dead. There was no way to save 'em when they'd eat a mess of it.

Laurel would give 'em "tackstomach," we called it. They held 'em and poured 'em down about a pint of linseed oil.

Then when they'd lose their cud, the way they'd fix their cud was to cram a dishrag down, or get 'em to eat one.

They'd usually, if they wasn't awful sick, they'd eat a dishrag; and in about thirty minutes, they'd be chewing their cud.

Ray Hicks, 1922 Watauga County

Injured Stock

If a horse got hurt, cut, or something, you'd just go out and restrain it, tie it, and then sew it up.

I remember one time down here, my father-in-law had a nice horse. He was going downgrade, going down to the barn. He stepped on a stick, and it flew up and hit him right underneath. Just laid open his internals, you know.

Well, we put them back; sewed him up. But he lived about two days and died. Infections, you know. We didn't have no veterinarians. You just had to do the best you could. Splint their legs. Do something if you could to try to help 'em, but in so many cases, you'd lose 'em.

George Perkins, 1916 Mitchell County

The Robin at the Milk Gap

There come a robin.
A beautiful robin would set on the stake,
the gap stake,
right at my milk gap
and sing to me.
It'd come to sing its song to me
every morning and evening.
And it liked to hear me sing.
It'd come to hear me sing.

And so I finally got on out with the other boys. They showed me how to build a flip shot, a slingshot — some called 'em a flip shot — out of the old red inner tube that was in the Model T and the A Model Ford.

And then it come on up to World War II, and they made synthetic rubber. And you ain't got a inner tube no more that you can build one out of. It ain't got no flip. It's got a little, but it flips slow, and they can get away.

But that red rubber, now, would kill 'em quick. The rock went so fast. Reminds me of that time back there in the Bible where David killed Goliath with his sling, that flip sling he had then. One of them where you put a rock in it, one piece of leather loops around your wrist, and the other end was loose, and you held it with your thumb. And you come around there and throw; and, boy, you could hit straight with that, and that's the way he hit through the armor of Goliath.

And so I got out with the other boys, and they learned me how to make a slingshot. One morning — or one evening, I forgot which one it was — I sighted at my robin there. I'd just take a shot at it. I didn't want to kill it. I just wanted to shoot at it with my slingshot, and, doggone, I killed it!

I sat down and cried. Never did nary nother one come back. That was all the one that ever got used to me, that'd do that. I hoped another one would come back, and I'd never shoot it. I throwed my slingshot down and never did carry another one.

Then, we was teached with our conscience not to kill little birds unless it was a mean bird.

And, you know, I studied over that. That bird, it took up corn. And the crows, they ain't mean; that's the way God created 'em. They don't know they're mean, them little chipmunks, picking corn up.

But they [other boys] had me believing they was mean. And the mockingbird, it would take up corn. They said to kill all the mean birds with the slingshot, but not to kill the robin and the sparrow and the snowbird and all the little harmless birds. Leave them and not tear their nests up. And you know it was a song:

"If I was a little bird, I tell you what I'd do;
I'd build my nest in a tall willow tree
Where the bad boys couldn't tear it down ... "

Did you ever hear that? I'd sing that.

My brother, he'd get him a slingshot, and it didn't bother him to kill. He'd go to the robins' nests where they was setting on their eggs, and he could hit so good with the slingshot that he'd shoot the top of their head off, it sticking up out of the top of their nest. Shoot it off of the nest!

Ray Hicks, 1922 Watauga County

What I Know of Animals

Now, here's the way it is. If you get too brave, you'll get killed or hurt or ruin your life. Get too brave.

Now, what caused people back yonder to suffer a lot, and caused me to suffer till I learned, was teached me of bears. I met bears pickin' blackberries.

And now there's some way, now, with a animal. I can't help but believe in me that a animal won't hurt me. They feel that, that I won't hurt them.

And I met this black bear pickin' blackberries. They eat berries, bears do. And I met it back there pickin' sweet blackberries and seedin' 'em. Briars tore down.

And me and my sister was pickin', and she was way around from me. I heard this a-comin' and thought it was her comin' around, a-meetin' me.

And when it come around, it was a big, black bear. It stopped close to me as that door there. Boy, it'd a-weighed four or five hundred pounds! Gosh! Its hair a-shinin'.

And the way it held its head. Yeah, it was pretty. So, at once it hit me that it might want to hurt this little boy. And I just said, "Bear," I says, "I love you. You won't hurt me."

It just stood there a while. And I just stood there. Then it just turned around and went back. Left me a-standin' there with my berry bucket.

Now, if I'd a-throwed that at it, now, that's the way people gets hurt. Throwin' a stick or rock at it. Usually, they'll pick up a rock cause there's plenty of rocks in these mountains. Hit it! Hit it in the head and maybe it'll hurt it. Then, it'll get you if it's hurt.

And I met another 'un [bear] down yonder, comin' one night in a old mountain road. It was an old wagon road that this house lumber was hauled up when Dad and my grandfather, his dad, hauled it up with a yoke of steers. They got this lumber down yonder off of that rough mountain when it was ice and snow. And he sawed it, and then they hauled it up this old wagon-steep road. Built this house.

And I met this bear down there that night on this road. It was still showing a little light. And I said, "Now, is that a bear or is it somebody a-rollin' a stump or something off the road?"

I kept easing a little closer and a little closer. (I'd seed a bear before, and I knowed how they looked.) He was a dark 'un. And I says, "No, that's big, black bear. Probably the one that I've seed before."

And so I just stopped in my tracks five, maybe ten, feet from him. It a-lookin' at me, and me a-lookin' at it. So I could tell of its actions that it seed I was scared. If I'd start to run, that'd build it up just like a bitin' dog. And it would have caused it to kill me.

See, it was a coward. Now, a little coward, if it sees it's bluffed somebody, it just builds it on up, and it'll just say, "I'll just kill you." Dogs is that way.

I said, "Well, I can't run. It's dark, and in this thicket I can't run. If it's gonna get me, it'll just have to get me."

Well, I'd read this story in school about Davy Crockett, where he'd grinned a coon to death. And I remembered what it said about him a-fightin' a grizzly. Now, a grizzly bear, they tell me that they're a lot worse than a black bear. Said Davy tried to grin the grizzly out, and it jumped on him. He cut it. He was stout, a big, stout young man that knowed every way of fightin'. So he cut the grizzly and saved his life. Killed him.

So I thought of that,
and I just stood and smiled.
In the dark.
And it would wiggle,
wiggle that way,
turn its head and look that way
and look back at me.

And I thinks to myself,
I believe that bear's gonna
tackle me yet.
Directly,
it'd just ease a little,
just like it was easing
a little toward me.

But I didn't move.
I just stood there.
Directly,
it turned its head
and looked out to the left of me.
And there was an old water break there
where we had cut it
to keep from washing the old road away.
And it just creeped
and turned away
and went out through the woods.

And I watched it go out through the woods,
leaves rattling,
twigs breaking.

It went on out.

Now, I'll tell you. It's like that with snakes or anything. Honeybees. If you'll use the wisdom that you can take from God and all the things he created. But there's about one out of a hundred will get you, no matter what you do.

But now, that's the way it is with snakes. Snakes don't want to bite if you'll leave 'em alone. But there's one, like I said, now and then, and it don't want to hurt you. Usually, you can get by it if you'll leave it alone.

It's a sheddin' its hide, and it's got its hide down over its eyes, and it will fight blindfolded if it hears something comin' up on it. Can't see.

And that's the reason snakes bite. They're scared. But usually, if you'll stand back, even if it's over their eyes, they won't hurt you.

If they don't smell that fear in you that you're going to hurt them. Now, the way God fixed it, they can smell that, or wind it some way or another from your body that you will kill them, that you will kill everything that you run on that you're a-feared of.

As long as I killed every little snake, say, "I'll get shet of you; you might hurt somebody else. You'll be gone!" That thing raised back. You couldn't kill 'em all.

And then it hit me that when I got to where that I don't kill a snake, a snake will lay and love me. It won't pay a bit of attention, just lay there. Look at me, but it won't bother me.

I don't bother them. I don't touch them. I just stand there and look at 'em. Directly, most of 'em will just crawl off right easy. Don't bother me atall.

Now, honeybees and a dog, most of 'em can tell. Unless it's one of them real mean ones that's been hit so much by people. And that's the way a snake is that's lived, where people have hit it, and it's lived. Where they didn't get it killed. It got well. Well, from then on, it don't take no chances. It'll bite you before you even know it.

But a snake or a dog that nobody's messed with, I ain't a-feared of none of 'em. I ain't afraid of being with none of 'em.

Now, a bee won't sting me. Now, a-robbin' the bees, if I don't mash on 'em, don't happen to mash on 'em, they won't sting me atall. But if I happen to mash 'em, they don't understand that, and they think I'm trying to kill 'em.

Now, you mash one, and the others will sting you. You mash that one, and they smell it — they smell that stuff that's inside — and they'll cover you black! Eat you up! They'll get around your neck. I've robbed 'em without a veil or anything. If I don't mash none, I don't get a sting.

Ray Hicks, 1922 Watauga County

The Cry of a Panther

Back in the old days they walked everywhere. And my grandmother had been sent to a neighbor's house for something. She was wearing an apron and a bonnet and a shawl. During that time they had a lot of panthers that were on the mountains.

And she started back through the woods, and she heard the cry of a panther. She started running. But the panther was gaining on her. So she had understood that all a panther would do would be to get the odor of the person. If you dropped a piece of clothing, it would stop to tear up that clothing before it went on.

So she dropped her bonnet. And then later, she dropped her shawl. Then she dropped her apron.

By that time she was climbing over a rail fence, and she got away. The panther didn't follow her on home.

She was frightened. She was only about twelve years old, she said.

I never did hear of anybody ever being attacked by a panther, but I know they were all frightened of them. I heard those tales even as I grew up. We were very frightened, even of a wildcat's cry—we thought maybe it might be a panther.

Pearl Randolph, 1912 Yancey County

Elk

Now,
Elk Park,
I would say,
actually,
also got its name from elk.
Because Banner Elk did, too.
There was actually elks—
and large ones!
Now, the elks and Banners
was what give Banner Elk its name.
The family of Banners.
Now
all the elks are gone.

Doyle I. Oakes, Sr., 1909 Avery County

Foxhunting

I started foxhunting when I was about eleven years old. Something like that. And we'd go out yonder on that bluff peak and lay out there all night long and listen to them dogs run.

Sometimes go on to the Flat Rock mountain. Stay all night and come back in up in the day the next day and lay down and rest a while and go on in to the cornfield or the sawmill or wherever we'd go to work. Nobody paid it no mind.

Now, we'd take about two nights a week foxhunting. And I kept that up for I don't know how long.

When I was fourteen years old, I worked in a logging camp in Coon's Creek. That's in Wilkes County. I worked in there for, oh, a couple of years. When I come out of that, I went to cuttin' timber then, for myself. I was on my own at that time. I followed cuttin' timber there for several years, foxhunting all the time.

I kept my dogs in a lot. I'd go out there, and I'd open the gate. I'd turn them dogs out and start them back to the mountain yonder. And I'd come and get in my car and go around the mountain to get on top.

By the time I'd get to the far end up there, they'd go through there, just about two or three mile on top.

Then they'd strike, and I'd be up there where I could hear every little crumb, almost. Now, when they "strike" is when they hit the track, when they scent the fox. Then they go to barkin'; but up to then they just keep quiet.

The one that goes to barkin' when they're comin' after 'em [before the strike] is what they call a babbler. Any fox hunter'd shoot one of them. We'd just kill it and be done with it.

I could tell every one of my dogs. I don't care how many dogs was in that bunch, I could tell my dog's mouth, voice different from any of 'em. And Clete Choate had one, and I had one that was just outstanding. That was all there is to it!

Yeah. They're clear. Some of 'em, clear. Some of 'em has a more of a throaty, some throaty voice; the majority of 'em has a clear-cut tone.

And the harder they run, you could tell it if you was a-listenin' at all, the harder they run, the better it sounds because it seems like the voice is actually bein' knocked out of 'em by their leaps, you know.

I had one had a bawling voice.
Then, he'd chop it up:
"Baooooo-oooo-oo-oo!"
Man alive!
That'd jerk you off the ground!
That was all there was to it.

And when they're all running together
on the scent of that fox,
man,
it's just one roar, that's all.
You can tell yours.

You can distinct the mouth of each dog.
They's just a little difference there.

Now,
I have knew mine and Clete's
to run as much as eleven hours.
When they got to the house here,
Buddy,
they'd lay down,
and you didn't have to worry about 'em
for a day.
It was just like you'd shot 'em.
When you'd feed 'em,
they'd just lay there.

No, never did have one to run itself to death. I've had 'em to run, to start in at the front part of the night and run till twelve o'clock the next day.

They run the fox in a hole. When it takes a notion to tree, it'll go in the hole.

Now, that mother fox
that's got the little cubs,
the dogs get after her,
and when she passes by that den,
you hear her bark
for them to get in the house!
That's a warnin' to 'em.

You hear the fox bark, too.
Just like a feist dog bark,
a feist,
a little bitty feller,
high-toned and sharp.
But they won't bark
unless it's a female with cubs.
They'll pass every once in a while, too,
Buddy.
When you're runnin' one of 'em,
they'll pass by that hole.

Get them baby dolls in the house!

Yeah, they sometimes catch 'em. Just tear 'em all to pieces. Now, a gray fox, I have killed a few of them. 'Cause they're hateful to run, anyway. They just get in the bush just like a rabbit. Run around and around. The dogs can't run 'em.

But what you do is you just go up on top of the mountain, and you just sit there and listen to it. I couldn't explain to you just how interestin' it would be to you just to stand and listen to them dogs. You know when anything is puttin' its heart into anything, like you are right there now; you're puttin' your heart in what you're doing. You can tell that.

All right, that's just exactly the way that the dogs are to runnin' when they're trailin' fox. From when they first strike to when they get up there, why, there's just as much difference in the sound of that as they is from day and night.

And I have thought the fox enjoys it.
Sure enough, I have.
I've heard foxhunters say
that certain foxes have really laughed
at the dogs.
You take one, say,
that's gonna be a-comin'
up through the field yonder.
If he's got just a little distance
between him and the dogs,
he can run around,
make just one great, long leap or two,
and the dog'll run by it.
And then it'll turn back.
Them poor old dogs'll run
plumb to the top of the mountain
and circle a half a dozen times
before they find out where it went.
Yes, ma'am.
Shut their mouths right there!
That's what is enjoyable
because it tries 'em out
to see just what a fox dog
really is.

Now, on the trail, it's every one of them tryin' to outrun the other one. I had one, I'd give a man a hundred dollars every time anything got ahead of it for the rest of the night. She'd shut her mouth that quick!

Next time she opened it, there wouldn't be nothin' ahead of her but the fox, and there wouldn't get nothin' else ahead of her but the fox, either.

Yeah, they fight each other. Just fight all the time. That's what makes it so interesting. They're every one tryin' to outdo the other one, you know. And you can tell it by the tone of the voice. That's right.

I think the dogs are actually enjoyin' the race. I do. When the race is over, and the fox goes in the hole, they just stop and come right straight to you.

Now, they's a lot of deer in here, but the majority of 'em won't run a deer. I don't know how they do it, but that deer just absolutely can lose that bunch of dogs right in the middle of the field.

Now, they's a lot of dogs that's got a better nose than others. Some of 'em's very keen scented, and some of 'em's common. You can take a dog that's very keen scented, and you can let a fox come through here when it's cold, and that dog will follow it. Now, when it's hot, it won't leave a scent as long as it does when the ground is cold.

Millard F. Pruitt, 1911 Alleghany County

Snake Tales

When I first bought this place, it had all growed up around the house, and me and my wife had to come over here and clean up around it so we could get in it. It was chock full of black-snakes. The house — in all these closets — the blacksnakes had went up these ratholes.

And I'm telling you the truth! We's in the bed one night, and something got cold, real cold around my feet. I said, "What've you got in this bed, Hon?"

She said, "Nothing."

I said, "The hell! There's something cold as ice."

She said, "There ain't nothing."

But I kept a-kicking it. It'd move. I'd kick it, and the dern thing would move. And I said, "I'm going to get up and turn the light on. There's something in this bed."

She said, "Ain't nothing in it."

So I got up, and when I raised up the covers, there was a dad-gummed old blacksnake! It was coiled up around my feet.

Well, I just took him. I fool with snakes. And if you grab one quick, a rattlesnake or anything, copperhead or anything, and give it that, you'll break its neck. I just grabbed that 'un and when I flipped it, I jerked its head off. I mean, just jerked it smack off! Like a whip. Yeah, like a whip.

So I throwed it out the door, and she said, "I ain't staying here no more."

"Well," I said, "just go somewheres else till I get 'em out of here."

So then later, I brought her brother's little girl and we raised her, you know. One of my wife's brother's little girls. Sent her to school. So she called me Tom all the time. Tom Stanley is my name. So she said, "Tom, there's something in the closet, and it'll come out. Must be a rat or something. And when I go in there, it'll go back."

Well, I kept a-watching, but I couldn't see a thing in there, not nary thing there.

So I told my wife, "You keep a watch and see what that young'un is a-seeing." And it was this blacksnake. It would smell cooking and stuff and come out. And when she'd open the door and see it, she'd slam it and run back.

So I got my .22 rifle, you know. And I said, "When you see it, Honey, just back away. Don't say a thing; don't shut the door. Just come to me."

Well, I was out in the yard, and she come. Said, "Tom, the mouse is in there."

Well, when I went in there, that thing, you know, that tongue a-flicking! So I fired, and I heard something fall in the other room. Crash! I said, "Gosh!" I got the snake and drug it out. And I said, "You'd better go in the other room. There's something broke."

So my wife said, "You shot my lamp in there on the dresser." But I got the blacksnake!

So I went on and went on a long time, and I got 'em out of the house, and I stopped all but about ten of the holes. Got the house fixed up.

And I was down here cutting corn in the fall of the year, and I heard that automatic rifle—"ting-ting-ting." And I knowed it was something bad because my wife wouldn't have been firing that thing. So, son, I had my pistol, and I run as hard as I could and come in to the house. When I got there, she was down at the chicken house a-shooting.

Went down there, and she was shooting blacksnakes. They'd go in there and get this egg in their mouth, swallow it, and then they'd go through a knothole and bust it.

That's the way they do it. And, if they ain't got a knothole to bust it with, they'll take and coil up like they're going to tie a knot and bust it.

And the next year after that I found two—and you can believe it or not; it's the God's truth—they started swallowing one another's tails. Each snake had swallowed up as far as they could and they both was dead. Both of 'em was swallowing each other.

Now, another one, see, my wife stayed over in Bate's Creek, and they had cradled, cut, oats. You know, they'd built a rail outfit to stack 'em on. So the old stuff was high. And it had growed up with grass in it. They wanted me to cut the grass. So I went up there to look at it.

And this is the truth. It ain't no joke. It's a fact! I don't know if you've ever heard of a stinger snake or not. A hoop snake. It rolls—a stinger on the end of its tail, and it's got a joint in it just like your finger. I was up there, and that thing would stick up this way and just disappear.

And I fit it till the sweat was rolling off of me. It was sometime the first of August. And I fit that thing until finally at last I made a lick at it and got it!

You can believe it or not, now, but Preacher Monroe—he's dead now—and a lot of 'em seen it. Its head was slick, just as slick as it could be, as any snake. And it was fine hair, just as fine, all over it. You could rub your hand over it, and it was just like rubbing a hog breast.

And that there joint there, nobody around here had ever seen one like it before. I wish I had cut it off and saved it. It was just like a bone. It could stick that in the ground and stand straight up. Stand up straight, just as straight as you're standing.

They call 'em "stinger snakes." We hung it up there till it rotted and dried. People would come from everywhere to see it. Its hair was short; I mean, you could rub your hand over it and feel it. And it could stand straight up, and its head would come out like that [demonstrates].

When I'd strike at it, it would disappear, get back down under some stuff. Then it would stick its head out somewheres else.

Stanley Hicks, 1911 Watauga County

The Habits of Snakes

But in the woods, we had more snakes then, see? We had the rattlers up here then. See, we had the timber rattlers. But after I moved, after my time, I can't remember seeing none. But my mother's dad, she said, killed 'em right up yonder where they was going to hoe corn. And we ain't hardly got a one anymore, nor any copperheads.

But we never did have any copperheads up on the mountain. They was all along the water where they could get frogs. And, too, they couldn't stand the cold that the rattler could stand. That's another thing that I studied — that we don't have the snakes anymore that we used to have because the time is come that we ain't got no frogs. And snakes won't stay where ain't frogs to swallow.

What we've got, anymore, of rattlers and copperheads is where I've been out gathering herbs along the watercourse, up a little from it, in a valley, where what few frogs there is here stays. Nothing ain't going to stay where they ain't no water and nothing to eat. We are going to hunt for something to eat if there is any chance to find it — and water.

Now, there was a place over yonder that was old-timey. Talk of rattlers and more copperheads! So I was a-gatherin' herbs, and these old men down the river said, "Ray, if you go in there, you won't live to get out. You'll be eat up with snakes." And I went all in there and never did see a snake of no kind. And then, finally, me and my boys was in there and seed a few of these here — they run in a den of these here little brown snakes. I was bit by one of them. Well, it hurt and swelled my ankle a little.

Ray Hicks, 1922 Watauga County

Blacksnakes

Now, there's blacksnakes around here. One morning I went into the kitchen and opened a door to come into the room there. And when I opened that door, there was a big old blacksnake a-layin' right on top of the door, and it fell down on top of my head!

I had an old mop a-settin' there, and there was a little back porch there, and I opened the door and got the mop and just mopped him right out into the yard! He crawled off. I didn't kill him.

One time we had a springhouse out there. Shady. Had two spring-run troughs in there. And we'd milk the cows and skim the milk and make butter and sell it.

And so one day my mother told me to do something here at the house, and she'd go churn. She always sat on the nail keg. So when she got done churnin', she moved the keg, and there was a big blacksnake under it. She'd been settin' on that snake all the time. I heard her hollerin' for me to come and bring the hoe.

Well, I went down there, but we never got the snake.

Hazel Campbell, 1893 Ashe County

Chapter 8. The Community

Even though mountain areas were sparsely settled, neighbors were cherished. In the days prior to modern social programs, any help one received in time of crisis came from friends and relatives. For the highlanders, giving such help was a matter of honor, and they would go to any lengths necessary to meet a neighbor's need.

Goods and services were readily exchanged, and it was a great day for peddlers. The cheerful little Irishmen came over the ridges from Tennessee and made their way into the homes and hearts of the mountain people.

Strict moral codes governed courtship. Young people did their "spooning" by the family fireside or riding to church together. Candy pullings and square dances lent a bit of excitement and merriment to their workaday lives.

Mountaineers have a natural love of music, and woodcrafting of musical instruments became a practiced art; the five-string fretless banjo was a favorite.

Never, however, were these folk hesitant about administering justice. Those who sought to take advantage of their fellowmen were punished, and swiftly.

Neighbors

People worked awful hard back in those days.
And people was good to each other then.
They loved each other.
If a family would get sick,
you know,
and if they had a crop that they were behind with,
why, the neighbors would all go in
and hoe that out and tend it and fix it.

And if they had to build a fence,
why, everyone went in and helped.

If they built a house,
it was the same way.
If they built a barn,
everyone went in.
And they enjoyed being together.
And whoever it was they were working for,
well, they would have a big dinner,
you know.
And the girls and women would come,
and we'd have a quilting.
While the men were working out, you know,
we'd have a quilting in the house.

Iowa Patterson, 1881 Clay County

The Sunday Visit

Y ou know, back then people would say, "I'm coming to see you, and I'm going to stay all day." Well, a lot of times on Sunday morning they'd start out with a wagon, and it'd take 'em two or three hours to go and two or three hours to come back, so they would stay all day. It wasn't like going someplace now and staying a few minutes. Staying all day was just a regular visit.

It didn't matter back then whether they let you know they was coming or not. They knew you'd be at home anyway. And, you know, most of the stuff was raised on the farm. Garden, plenty of wild meat. Didn't cost much.

Richard Childress, 1905 Avery County

Country Hospitality

Why,
you'd just leave your doors open
if you was a-going to go off somewhere.
Why,
you'd just go on!
Never think a thing about it.

And my daddy never turned nobody off.
Here'd come an old crap;
he'd just take him in.

Nannie Smith, 1888 Clay County

Honor

Back when I was comin' up with my father, your word went a long ways. If you promised somebody that you'd be there tomorrow morning to help 'em work, you'd be there. Or you'd be sick, and you'd usually try to let 'em know.

If you borrowed money, you didn't have to get a cosigner or someone to sign for you. You'd say, "I need to borrow fifty dollars." And the man would let you work it out or pay it back however you wanted to.

But you would pay it back. Usually he would know you. People would borrow from one another then.

My father bought a milk cow, and he paid seventy-five dollars for her. And he was only making a dollar a day working. And so he worked this cow out with that man. Paid him seventy-five dollars.

But the man knew him, knew that he was honest. And he knew that he'd be there to pay for the cow. If you didn't have the money, why, you worked for the people.

Ralph Crouse, 1922 Alleghany County

A Right Smart of Difference

Well, as for courting, there was a right smart of difference a-courtin' then and there are now. Well, I had a couple of sisters older than I was. The two oldest of the family was the sisters. They would dress up to go to meeting. Now, they'd put on their long dresses down below their shoe tops. The people back then wore shoes. There wasn't any such thing as slippers. They wore high-topped shoes, buttoned up. They came up quite a little bit. And the sleeves came down to their wrists, and the neck buttoned right up under their chin. And all you ever seen of a woman was her face and hands.

They would put on what they called "hoops," great big things that come up around here and made their dresses stand out. And then they put on what they called a "bustle." It was a big pad on their hips back there. Homemade ones. They made them theirselves, you know. They thought it made them look better, you know. I was too little to know much of what the men thought about them then.

Well, the young fellows went to see their girls a-foot. Once in a while, one would have something to ride. Well, they had mules. We, at home, always had a team. We had to have a team to work. So far as going out of a Sunday, they generally had a mule to ride. But sometimes, when they'd plow them mules all week, they'd let them rest of a Sunday because they was tired. And they'd take it a-foot, you know. Oh, they'd go three or four miles, and they'd dress up, but it was in mostly homemade clothes. But they went decent, all right.

They'd usually meet at church, and then they'd bring the girls home, you know. Stay sometimes till bedtime.

Henley Crawford, 1879 Clay County

Candy Stews

We'd have these dates,
you know,
and travel two or three miles
on foot.
That was nothing unusual.
We'd have a candy stew —
we called it a candy stew —
or we'd have a corn shucking
or some event,
such as grinding molasses,
to get together.

At the candy stew,
we'd make up a bunch of chocolate candy,
you know.
Milk, chocolate, sugar.
what have you.
Everybody would get around
and tell tales,
play games.

Have you a girlfriend.
Everybody would be paired off
with 'em a girlfriend,
usually.
And sometimes,
girls would come in
from other communities.
And we'd have a new girl
or a strange girl,
we'd call 'em.
She'd come in and talk.
Why,
everybody would be after
that particular one
till they become acquainted.

George Perkins, 1916 Mitchell County

The Fortune Teller

When the young people were courting, they'd go walking, have picnics on the river. A group would take their lunch, and then they would ride in a boat up and down the river, the New River.

Me and my husband went to an old fortune-telling woman, and we had planned that day to be married the next Sunday.

So when she told our fortune, she said, "Well, if you're not already married, you will be in a week."

No, she didn't know nothin', 'cause we just planned it as we went on.

She'd use a coffee cup to tell our fortunes. Take the grounds, turn the cup. She looked like a witch. She was old with gray stringy hair and kept five or six dogs.

I went to a fortune teller when I was over a-visitin' kinfolks. We walked, a crowd of us. And she told 'em by cards. My cousin and I and two others went; and she told my cousin, says, "You watch her. She'll get the dirt out from under your feet!"

So I got the boyfriend that she used to have!

When we were getting ready for our boyfriends, we'd curl our hair with a curling iron. Heat it over a lamp chimney and get it hot. Then we'd put "rats" in our hair. We'd take a stocking and stuff it full of cotton and put it around in a circle. Then we'd comb all our hair up to hide all that, and then put a big bow on top.

I think I had a bow that had four yards in it.

Then, we'd get our pictures made. They'd bring a black something they held over their heads and over the camera.

Ruth Sturgill, 1893 Alleghany County

The Proposal

I went to a farm school for a year of college, but then I come on back home to work with my daddy. Went to farming here again. Hard way of going.

Then I got into lumbering. Made good, or what was good then. Course, jobs were scarce, and I was just lucky to be on a job. There weren't many jobs.

Well, it come up time for us to get married. Me and Zeola was going together a little bit. And we decided to get married. But I didn't tell her when we was going to get married.

Well, we had talked it over. But I hadn't told her we was going to get married then. So one day I decided we was going to.

So I went to Elizabethton. I caught the bread truck. See, I didn't have any transportation.

So I caught the bread truck to Elizabethton and got my license to get married. And I come back down here and sent word over to her house that we was going to get married. To come over here.

She come over there, and I said, "Well, we're going to get married."

She said, "When?"

I said, "Tonight."

"Oh," she said, "Lord, no!"

I said, "Yeah, we're going to get married tonight."

Well, we run away and got married. Yeah, we sneaked away and went back to Elizabethton and got married and stayed gone about a week.

Then we come back here and started housekeeping. There was an old house up here. And we started housekeeping on seventy-five dollars. I bought our furniture and stove and whatever we had, which wasn't much.

But we had enough to cook with; we had enough bedding; we had enough to set on. And so on, lean up against.

Then after World War II, we bought this place. So we'd had this place about seven, eight, ten years; and we went off one day, and everything we had burned up.

Well, it was about another year before we got a house started out here at this place. Now I've been working at construction for the last thirty years, I guess.

But back in our early days, it wasn't just us that lived hard—everybody lived hard, or everybody in this area. Back during the twenties, thirties, up till the war started, there wasn't any money. No money and no work.

George Perkins, 1916 Mitchell County

Sharing

When I was born,
my mother was forty-six.
And my husband was born April the twenty-fourth,
and me,
August the twenty-fourth.
They lived over the hill from me.
And his mother was younger,
and she come to where I was born.
I was born at my home,
of course.
So she come and took me with my husband,
Clarence,
and divided food
for me and him that night
and kept me.
But we didn't even know each other for years.
Just knowed that he was Clarence
and me, Nannie.
And so, later then, we was married.

Nannie Smith, 1888 Clay County

Sunday Picnics

Back when we were young,
we'd have square dancing,
candy pullings.
When the syrup was made in the fall,
they always had a candy pulling
around the syrup mill.
They'd boil the syrup and pull it.
That was in the fall.
That was always a big occasion.
There were picnics.
We used to go to the mountains
to a fall
and have our picnics after church.
Wore dresses down to your shoetops.

Kate Hayes, 1892 Cherokee County

Rocking the Boys

And when we grew up,
we had parties and dances.
We entertained ourselves at home
with our friends.
We didn't get in cars and go
like they do now.

Well now,
the young people all gathered at our homes,
and the girls had boyfriends,
and when they went home,
they was rocked!
That is,
when the boys started home,
the other boys would rock them—
throw rocks at them!
They'd run!
Had to run for their lives!

It could be dangerous.
They didn't want to start home.
They had to walk.
Either walk or ride a horse.

Vastie Hensley, 1904 Yancey County

Telling Jokes

Old-time people,
they was always coming by
telling you a joke or a big story.
They'd get a kick out of it.
It kind of excited you,
and they'd get a kick out of it.
That was because
they didn't have other entertainment.

Mrs. Hettie Loven, 1899
Mrs. Pearl Marshall, 1904 Avery County

The Practical Jokester

Here in the mountains men played jokes on one another. And one winter somebody got a joke on this one man, and he decided he was going to come back with another one. He found snowshoes. Well, we didn't know what snowshoes were back then, you know.

Well, he put them on early one morning before daylight, and he walked across the mountain. He come to a branch, and then he'd just go into the branch and take off his snowshoes and walk up the branch.

So you'd come to the branch or creek and the footsteps wouldn't go any farther. There they'd be. Well, everybody thought it was some kind of monster after their sheep and cows and horses. So they got this manhunt out. They had everybody in the county they could get who farmed or had cattle out hunting.

See, there was just two of 'em that knew this. It was the man who had the snowshoes and the man who loaned them to him. And they let it

blow up pretty big. So finally the feller that did it come to the conclu-
sion that he'd better tell what it was.

So he told 'em that it was the snowshoes. Well, they didn't believe
him. So he had to show them what he did with the snowshoes.

This big foot was there in the snow. Well, it just went off into the
water and no sign of it after that.

Vastie Hensley, 1904 Yancey County

The Love of Music

Music.
The mountain people love it.
All of it.
And most of 'em
love all kinds.
They do a lot of dancing.

Lorene Dickson, 1908 Ashe County

Buck Dancing

I do buck dancing, mostly. Some square dancing. But they don't
dance no more like we used to do. They got too much of this here
fancy stuff.

Old-time dancing. It was much different than it is now. Back then you
tap danced. That is, the women. Women tap danced. Men buck danced.
Buck dancing is different from any other dancing you see. I don't know
as you ever seed any of it, but anyway, it's different. No. They didn't
know what clogging was then.

And they had square dances, but they ain't like the ones they do now.
They change 'em too much. Got too much of this here fancy stuff in 'em.
I mean, son, it's different, much different from what it is now. I couldn't
dance this new stuff they've got. It would tangle me up, and I'd be killed
at it. You know, all that there fancy—I call it fancy—but that's what
they've learnt and what they know.

Stanley Hicks, 1911 Watauga County

Homemade Banjos

I've got a dulcimer up there Dad made fifty-eight years ago, and I've got a banjo I made fifty-two years ago. I cut that finger off a-making 'em, and I had to change the way I played my banjo cause I didn't want to quit.

Old homemade banjo, when I growed up, didn't have no frets. What they made didn't have no frets. Well, a lot of people can't play now without 'em!

I cover the banjo head with a groundhog hide. I tan my own hides. I get my own groundhogs, tan my own hides, make my own skins. They've got so high you can't buy 'em. Cost about twelve dollars apiece.

Sometimes I can get three out of a groundhog, sometimes two, sometimes just one. It just depends on what size you have.

I've been making 'em, off and on, about fifty-two years. Dulcimers, I've made them about twenty years, off and on. Dad, he sold 'em, when he made 'em, for two dollars and a half. A banjo. And a dulcimer was three. Used a hand saw. I've still got it up in the shop. I'll show you.

Well, you had to do something back then to live, to survive.

Stanley Hicks, 1911 Watauga County

Trading at the Store

Take a dozen eggs or two or an old hen or a ham of meat, what-ever you have, and go to the store. It was just the same as taking money. Whatever the people that run the store would pay you for it is what you got.

Oh, they had live chickens, had a place to put the live chickens. And a wagon would come by the store and pick 'em up, pick up the ham of meat, corn, or grain, or whatever you had.

And that fellow would take 'em on over to Wilkesboro or bigger towns like that. Get rid of them there.

Just like the fur, you know. Animals. We used to trap animals here. Well, you didn't get much. Take a possum, now, you'd get ten or fifteen cents for a possum hide. And maybe a quarter for a muskrat. Sell rabbits for eight and ten cents apiece.

Rabbits, we used to take them to the store. Put 'em in a barrel. Had a great big barrel there. This is after you kill 'em and take the entrails out. Leave the skin on 'em.

Carry 'em to the store, and the man that runs the store, he'd send 'em somewhere else, then. He didn't keep 'em but four or five days, you know, in the wintertime. Have 'em in a fifty-five gallon barrel.

You'd carry chickens or hams
or whatever you had to the store,
and if you didn't use it all up
gettin' coffee and sugar and salt
and stuff you didn't raise,
why,
they'd give you a "due bill" for it.
They'd write you out a piece of paper
that they owed you, say,
two dollars and a half
for a ham,
and when you needed some more stuff
from the store,
why,
you'd have to take
this due bill back to the store
where you had let 'em have your ham.

That way you'd go back to the same store instead of going to another store. See, if they'd paid you the money, you might have wanted to go to another store.

Now, they kept most any kind of food and things in the store then. It was packaged different from what it is today. Altogether different.

Take side meat, what a lot of people now call bacon. You go to the store now, it's already sliced and packaged. Well, then they just cut off — if you wanted a pound or two pound — they just cut off as close as they could to that amount.

About everybody had their own coffee mill. You had to buy the beans and grind your own coffee. It's just that they didn't have the way of processing it then like they do today.

You could buy a pair of shoes for a dollar, dollar and a half. And they were very good shoes. My grandfather, he used to make shoes. Homemade shoes. Yes, ma'am, they were comfortable. Put together with solid leather.

Not any tacks, much, used in 'em. They used pegs. Maple pegs. Pegged 'em together.

And they had a little wooden last. I've got several of 'em scattered around here somewhere. And they used it something similar to the way we make shoes today. Only it was wooden.

They had a pattern to cut it out with. Course, they looked a little different back then, but they generally used the same pattern.

But back then, the people thought it was really something to get a pair of store-bought shoes, you know. But there wasn't too many people could make shoes.

Ralph Crouse, 1922 Alleghany County

The Peddler

Back when I was a little girl, people would travel around. They'd go with a pack on their back. Lots of 'em would walk, and lots of 'em would ride a horse.

Now, the ones with the packs on their back were a-sellin' something. Peddlers. Oh, yes. They'd stop at houses. Why, they've stayed all night at my daddy's house a many a night.

They'd bring tablecloths. And just small things, you know. Children's dresses. Awful pretty tablecloths! My mother bought some.

One time a peddler spent the night, and naturally, my mother wanted to strip the bed before anybody else could sleep there. And he had left his money! Under the pillow.

Oh, Lord! It scared her to death!

Said she went to the door. She wanted to see if there was any chance to get on a horse and catch him. But he come back. And she never touched a bit of it.

And when he come back, she met him at the door. And she said, "I went to make the bed and saw that there, but I didn't touch it." And so he got it.

Oh, he would charge twenty-five cents or fifty cents for a fine tablecloth.

They didn't carry nothing that was heavy but clothing on their backs, you know. They'd have a great big sack.

Tennie Cloer, 1886 Cherokee County

Buying Eyeglasses

The old peddlers
would bring eyeglasses along.
And you'd just keep trying them
until you could find a pair
you could see through.
And they would have needles
and embroidery hooks,
things that women would be interested in.

Thelma Penland Axley, 1906 Clay County

Getting the Mail Through

I can remember a time when we lived back here on this mountain they called "Peach Bottom Mountain." Back there the mailman rode a horse. And the snow would get higher than the fences. It melted a little and froze. So he could just ride right across the fences same as if they wasn't there. I can remember that very well.

Oh yeah, the mail usually got through. They had two mail carriers, and one would go one way, and the other one would go the other way. You see, two routes they'd take. Of course, if it was pretty weather, it'd just be one route. But in bad weather, they'd split it up. Two would usually get the mail through. It might be dark, about dark, when the mailman would come by, but he'd come.

And that sure was a cold job, riding a horse.

Ralph Crouse, 1922 Alleghany County

The Post Office at Home

Now, this is Tomotla, an Indian name. That was the old post office. But it's no longer a post office. No longer at Tomotla. Most people, you tell 'em we live at Tomotla, and they'll know where that is.

There's no *m* in the Indian language. It's *w*. And Tomotla should have been Tow*otla*. That's what so many people misunderstood.

My grandfather was postmaster, and when he went into the Civil War, this post office was discontinued for two years. Then his son took it over. George W. Hayes, Jr. And he left, and my father, when he become twenty-one, became postmaster. He was the second oldest postmaster in the United States in years of service when he ended. Forty-eight years.

And when he was no longer postmaster, my sister took it. They had the post office right here in this house. They had it, not right here in this room, the living room, but in what is a bedroom now on the other side.

This part of the house has been added. The front of the house—what they thought was the front then—was built in 1850. This part was built later.

Slaves' quarters stood down on this side. The old slave houses. And the main highway was on the back side, what was the front then.

But when the railroad came in 1885, they took part of the yard and what was then the highway, and they had to move the highway over for the railroad.

So the train comes right behind the house. We used to have four a day. Two passengers and two freights. But we only have one train a day now. Freight train.

The first mail was brought on horseback back in 1860, '61, and up till the train come in. It came first to Franklin from Asheville. And then it came to Andrews. And the man came on horseback, summer or winter.

And they'd say when he got here, in the wintertime, that his feet were sometimes frozen to the stirrups. And they'd have to help him down by knocking the stirrups loose from his boots.

And they only had one mail a week.

I can remember when the train brought the mail. Later, the train would come about ten o'clock at night, and they'd set up to get the newspaper.

Now,
the mail train passed
right in front of the house.
And there was a crane that was built up,
and there was an arm,
an iron arm on the crane.
And, as the train passed,
he threw the mail bag off,
and the hook caught the bag.
And it fell on the ground.

As the mail hit the ground,
we had a dog—
a big, black shepherd—
that landed on the mail bag
by the time it hit the ground.
He just stood there till someone,
some member of the family,
came to get the mail.
Wouldn't let a stranger touch it.

He wasn't trained.
He just came here.
He was a stray,
just came.
And he was later killed
by a passenger train.

Kate Hayes, 1892 Cherokee County

Old-time Photographers

It was hard traveling, trying to get around in the mountains. You know, part of the roads was just trails. Just wagons. Rough. But, back then, where we lived, on the head of Pigeon Roost, there was somebody traveling through there all the time. Pigeon Roost, that was where I was born and raised. Been moved away from there twenty years.

Yeah, I can remember. People traveled all the time; it was a passways through there to Tennessee. And sections on through there, Bean Creek and Poplar. There was somebody traveling through there every day.

Well, come through there selling things. Sold medicine. Bring medicine. And take pictures, you know. Enlarged. I can't remember it, but I've heard my older sister talk about it; they come two men in a buggy.

Part of 'em was gone. My daddy and mother was there, and most of the children. They took a picture of us, and when they delivered it back, we didn't have the money. And they wouldn't let us have it without the money, and they took it away and give it to somebody.

And then the family heard of it and went for it. But they charged so high they couldn't pay for it. And they never did get it.

I've heard my sister say she'd give anything in the world for it. Oh, it wasn't too much, but money then was hard to get. I don't reckon it was over two or three dollars. But, see, we couldn't get that much money. Even the neighbors, everybody, was broke.

See, it was a long time after they took it that they come back, but we just couldn't get the money.

Harvey J. Miller, 1909 Mitchell County

Poling across the River

I grew up on the South Fork
of the New River.
And the only way to get across
was with a boat.
And we had people
who would come to one side
of the river and call,
and you'd take the boat over to 'em.
Or,
if you were on the other side and called,
they'd have to bring it back to you.

Well,
it was a flat-bottomed boat
that you used a pole with
to pole it across.
And in the wintertime
when the mush-ice would run,
you'd have to go up the river
and kind of angle it across,
or you couldn't make it.
That was when it would be so cold
that the water would be freezing,
and the river would be full of ice.
The ice would be soft,
but it would push the boat
down the river too far
unless you faced it
and went up the river
and then angled it across.

And then we'd land
at what we called the boat landing.
We had a certain place
that we could land the boat,
and you could get in and out.
But,
once in a while,
the river would get so high
that no one would try to cross it,
anyway.

Mildred Torney, 1918 Alleghany County

The Esseola Inn

O h, they used to have a Esseola Inn at Linville as far back as I can remember. They'd come in there to the depot, and they'd have folks to meet these rich people, mostly. They'd come in there and get big trunks and baggage. They had a big hotel over there. It finally got burned out. It was called Esseola Inn.

They'd travel to the depot on the train; then they'd meet them in buggies and surreys and ever what they had. Wagons. Take 'em over to the hotel. They would stay all summer. That was around 1900.

Richard Childress, 1905 Avery County

When the First Train Came

W hen my mother first came up to Murphy, she found out that she had to jump rocks to get across the street, to get out of the mud.

And about that time, the first train was coming to Murphy. But it didn't come all the way in. At that time they had what they called the "Old Depot."

My father was a lawyer, and he had to go to the Supreme Court for a case. And you know, back then it would take all week and sometimes ten days to go, because the railroad didn't come to Murphy this way.

You had to go, use your horse and buggy up to where it came on the Southern Railroad. And then trains and transportation was just slow.

So, as soon as he was to return, the railroad was to come in, first train. And they had asked him to be the speaker. So he asked my mother to please write him a speech while he was gone.

Well, you know how flowery they used to write them. So she spent all the time he was gone writing his speech. And the morning they had it — I don't remember whether it was to be a barbecue or a picnic or dinner on the ground or what — but people began coming in about four o'clock. And they were tying their horses and mules and teams to the different trees over in what we used to call the "Old Cut Depot."

And when that little narrow-gauge engine started around the hill blowing the horn, all the mules and the horses took off up the hill! And the owners had to go after them.

So when all the excitement was over, my father and a few of the other VIPs were the only ones left on the station platform to hear his speech.

And Mama said that was the most wasted time she had ever spent. Nobody heard all her big words!

Emily Cooper Davidson, 1894 Cherokee County

Reducing the Dollar

I can remember back
when they cut the size of the dollar bill.
I can remember hearing the people say
that the country was really
going downhill fast, now.
We didn't have enough paper
to make a dollar bill with.

Cut 'em to the size they are now.
I have one of the big dollar bills.
They was about twice as large.

Ralph Crouse, 1922 Alleghany County

Justice

When anybody murdered anybody here,
they really wanted to put 'em behind bars.
And,
if the law needed any help,
why,
it wasn't any trouble
to get help to put 'em behind bars.
And then,
if they were guilty,
they believed in puttin' 'em to death.

Ralph Crouse, 1922 Alleghany County

Hangings

Now, back in them times, they just handled law theirselves. If they stole a horse or anything, they just had a tree and they hung 'em. They took and hung 'em. That's what they done with 'em.

Now, if they done anything very mean or anything, they had a man, an old feller who was a magistrate. They'd take 'em there and try 'em. And then, if it was too bad, they'd send 'em to Birmington, somewhere off down there and keep 'em in jail.

But if it wasn't too bad, they'd let 'em pay what little amount it was, if they had stole corn or chickens or anything like that. Oh yes, they was arrested and brought in to a magistrate and tried.

Now, I never did see the hangings, but I've heard Grandpa talk about 'em. He'd been to 'em. He said they were pretty pitiful. They'd take and put 'em on a horse, and then they slapped the horse and it'd run out from under them. And that was it.

He said he saw two fellers hung. My great-grandpa, he was down there when they hung Tom Dooley.

My grandpa took me and went to where he was hung at. It was on a white oak tree down this side of Wilkesboro. Then they carried him from there to Darby to bury him. They carried him, I'd say, around eight miles from where they hung him at.

And he didn't kill this woman. See, he took the blame on hisself. He was courtin' both of 'em. Two women. Tom Dooley was. And so one of 'em wanted to get rid of the other 'un.

And he helped dig the grave after she killed her. She killed this woman herself—stabbed her with a knife. But he took the blame on hisself. He didn't kill her atall, but he did that to keep the other woman from being killed.

Yeah, that's true! I went to the tree where he was hung at. Grandpa took me down there when I was very small, and I saw the tree. It was in level country, the best I can remember. It was a white oak tree, and it was dying. I mean, some of the branches was dying on it.

And he said, "Now, right there is where they hung Tom Dooley at."

Stanley Hicks, 1911 Watauga County

Frost on His Head

A man was hung on the Franklin bridge right close to home. He worked for Miss Penland. She was a fine woman; everybody loved Miss Penland. She was so good.

So this man worked for her for five years. One night he went in on her. He was trying to gag her and get her money. But he didn't kill her. He just bruised her up.

But they heard her, you know. And they never waited for that man to have a trial! They never waited for nothing! The men grabbed him up and slung him up on that bridge at ten o'clock at night. And he was a-hangin' there the next morning with frost on his head!

And I always felt funny when I come along there, going across that bridge. I'd look up, a-thinkin' about where they hung that man.

Tennie Cloer, 1886 Cherokee County

Feuds

Feuds? Lord, yes! We had a place up on Pigeon Roost; that's what gave it a notorious reputation. Back there in World War I, the bad men stayed there. Made moonshine whiskey. People still, now, you tell 'em about Pigeon Roost, and they've heard of that place. That was a bad place.

You know, they've killed men there. Made liquor there. And big men, they've traced 'em. Notable fellows, they'd travel through there. And when they'd get there, they'd just get swallowed up. Never could trace 'em no more.

There's a place back there now they call Dead Man Hollow, where there was so many of them men buried. Yeah, the law would go in there and have a shoot-out.

See, an old man was raised back there. He stayed at home. And there was a preacher that went through there going to Tennessee. Had a church over there.

Their wives was kin to each other. And the old man told that preacher that he had so many crocks full of money, you know. That preacher told him, "Now, you've made a lot of money. My advice to you is to sell out, sell your place here, take that money, and to go off and put it into something. Get out of North Carolina. I hear they're going to come in on you and put you out of business. You ought to go down to Tennessee and buy you a good place and start new."

And the old man said, "No, preacher. I want to make a few more dollars. I'm going to do what you say, but I've got to make a few more dollars first."

Well, you know it wasn't but a little bit till the law got him and took him to court. And when he come out, they had took his money, you know. Found his cash.

And he said, "Preacher, I'm broke."

The preacher said, "I told you that you'd better move out."

Now, that old man got his money from making liquor. Now, his wife was kind of religious.

Yeah, they sent him three months on the road one time. He come back. And they lived to be old.

That old woman told me that she'd seen haints, ghosts, out there at that house. And they was the most restless people I've ever seen. Seems like they couldn't be still. They was always a-watchin' like, you know?

We'd be on the porch, and that old man would jump up and peek down the road, and I'd say, "Are you expecting somebody?"

He'd say, "Yeah, the law is supposed to be here, through here today." People would tell him such things as that. He was old, you know.

I'd say, "The law?"

He'd say, "Yeah, the law!"

He quit making his moonshine, but his boy and grandson stayed on with it, kept it going. But he'd done got too old.

I went there one day, me and a man, and this old fellow was reading the Bible. He read his Bible out a-loud. We went in.

He said, "Have a chair, fellows. Let me read on some. It'll do you good to hear this." He'd read on, you know. Had an old Bible.

And he'd explain, too, you know. Like a preacher. It was interesting. And his wife — I went out on the porch — she's kin to me. I went out on the porch and talked to her, and she'd tell about them a-hearing things.

She said, "I'm worried."

I said, "What are you worried about?"

She said, "I seen a man up there to the grave field. I was up this morning, and it a-peeping daylight; and I seen a man a-standing up there, up there in the grave field."

There was a little field up the road there they called the "grave field."

She said, "I don't understand what he meant. He was standing there looking everywhere. Something is going to happen."

Then she told me, said, "We're hearing things."

You know, folks claimed people was killed there. Right there in that house, they claimed they was killed. Yeah, she had a lot of trouble, now. Lot of things to study about. They got old, you know. Seen and heard a lot of things. That was the way she was; she couldn't be still.

Harvey J. Miller, 1909 Mitchell County

"Firsts"

This is about my father, G. H. Haigler, of Hayesville. He was born in 1855, and he said that he remembered hearing the guns from Chattanooga during the Civil War. He wasn't big enough to, you know, take part, but he remembered hearing the guns.

And he remembered the first box of matches he ever saw. They came in little wooden boxes.

And that old saying, "What did you come after, a coal of fire?" if you are in a hurry — that was true! People kept a fire the year around, summer and winter. And if it went out, they had to go to the neighbors for a coal of fire, and they had to hurry with it! Or it would go out.

And my mother said she remembered the first candy she ever saw. Somebody married in Hayesville, and they had stick candy.

My father would be a hundred and twenty-three years old now, and my mother would be a hundred and sixteen, if they were living.

And they also told me about the salt. Salt was so hard to get. They had to go to Cleveland, Tennessee, for all their goods. You know, a man would take a wagon and go out for two or three days. And they'd camp on the way.

Then they'd bring back a little calico material and a little cloth goods, you know, as well as salt and sugar and things like that.

They had a smokehouse, and they'd hang the meat up and salt it well. And after it was through and had dripped, they'd take that stuff off. And they'd boil it and strain it and get their salt because they didn't have any.

You know, there aren't many people that know what a milk gap is. It's a kind of a fenced in little place. Maybe the cows are all in the pasture, and you call 'em in to milk 'em. And you get 'em in this little corral and feed them and milk them, you know. There's not many people who know what a milk gap is.

Kate Mauney, 1899 Cherokee County

Christmas

How'd
we
celebrate Christmas?
Oh,
feeding cattle.

Tom Pruitt, 1904 Alleghany County

Chapter 9. Mountain Stories

To the Carolina highlander, the telling of stories and legends is second nature. He needs only a conversational pause and the merest suggestion of a topic to begin an old yarn, usually one passed down from his dad or grandpa.

Geographical isolation, the heritage of Scotch-Irish and English traditions, and long winter evenings by the fireside have combined to cultivate this rich storehouse of oral culture. Youngsters and adults alike sit transfixed while their elders practice with devout dedication to perfect their "telling of the tale."

Herein is contained a verbatim account from the traditional Jack tales. No North Carolina collection would be complete without one. It came from the Hicks family, one of the several original sources of Richard Chase's recordings of these old tales.

The Molasses Story

Well, I'm a-gonna tell you a true tale that happened to us. This is a true story. It happened to me and my brothers. Had two older brothers. Right yonder's one of 'em's picture. That's the one just older than I am.

Me and him and my brother younger than I am was at home. Mother and Daddy took the other young'uns and went to stay all night and left us at home, us three there to look after the place, milk the cow, and take care of things.

So we made 'lasses at that time. Had two sixty-gallon barrels. Sixty-gallon wooden barrels. And we put these 'lasses in 'em. And we had this barrel setting right beside the stairsteps. We had a black cloth over it and a plank over it.

And this cat would be upstairs and hear a racket, and it would come down, down out of the loft, jump off the stairs, you know, on the barrel and then on the floor.

So, along that morning, we got up and got breakfast. We always eat molasses, and I don't know which one done it, but when we went to get the 'lasses out, we left the cloth off and the cover off of the 'lasses and went back and was eatin' breakfast.

Well, we just got started eatin' good, and I heard something go "Mee-oooowwww! Weeeeee-ooooow! Weeeeooooow!" Well, I went in there, and we had these 'lasses eat down, I guess fifteen gallons, at it, maybe twenty left in that barrel.

So I looked down in there. Just two big eyes was all I could see. Well, I got on the side of the barrel and reached down in there as far as I could and got it by the head, and I pulled it up.

Then I thripped it off. You know, take your hand and just thrip them 'lasses off. Just thrip down its tail real good. Then I run through the house. The 'lasses run through the house, too.

And then, see, we had a washblock outside. See, you battled your clothes out then. Well, I scrubbed that old cat the best I could on the old washblock. Got all the 'lasses out that I could. Then I turned it loose.

Then we went back to the house. Had to scour all that 'lasses up along the floor. We knowed they'd kill us—hang us, as far as that goes—if they knowed it when they come back.

Well, we scoured a streak from the barrel to the front door in the house. Just worked ourselves to death! But when we got through, there you could see it—just a clean streak from the barrel to the door. And we knowed Mother would kill us for sure if'n she seen that.

So we set in to scour the whole house! Cleaned it all out, scoured it all out good. And we kivered the barrel back up. Fixed it back.

Well, Mother come back, and she looked where we'd cleaned up the house. And she said, "Boys, I ain't got boys no more! They're men now! Just look where they cleaned this house up while we was gone. They've scoured it out and cleaned it up. I wouldn't take nothing for my boys now. They're men; they ain't boys."

Dad said, "Yeah, they just had to do something."

And so it went on. And suppertime come, and Mother wanted to do something real nice for us boys 'cause we'd been so good to scour her floor, so she baked up a big pan of biscuits and set out a fresh cake of butter and got out some 'lasses. We set down to the table, and I said, "Well, I don't want no 'lasses."

And Daddy said, "Well, what's the matter?"

I said, "Well, we got floundered on 'em. We just eat too many and got sick on 'em and don't want none." And I said, "Just give Grandma and Riley our part of 'em." Riley was our step-grandpa. They was there then.

So that went on a day or two, maybe three days. And this cat, now, the 'lasses had dried on it. And you know, an old cat, back then, would come and rub agin these old people and go, "Meeee-oooowwww," and they'd give it a piece of bread or something.

So he commenced it, and "Meeee-oooowww." But he couldn't get his tail up. He just raised it up partway, and it was right rough. Looked terrible bad.

Dad couldn't see too good, and he said, "What, in the name of goodness, has happened to that cat, Stanley?"

And I said, "I think John Moss's old dog's been a-chewing on it."

And he said, "I'll kill that dog if it's the last thing I ever do. I'll kill that dog."

And I said, "Well, I wouldn't kill 'im, but I think that's what done it."

Well, them 'lasses got gone. But before they got gone, John's old dog came up there. The old cat was around there, but he didn't bother the cat. But Dad went out there and killed him. He killed that dog.

And that went on and went on till after the 'lasses was gone. And then Daddy opened up another barrel, and we just went into 'em. Then Daddy said, "There's something wrong."

But I said, "No, we just got over that floundering spell."

And so we started eatin' on 'em. And that went on for years. Then one day we was up in the field, all of us. We was all grown then. And I got to thinking and got so dern good tickled about it. We'd got to telling tales and all, and I said to Dad, I said, "You never did find out about that cat and that old dog, did you?"

He said, "No, and I don't know that I want to."

"Well," I said, "I'm a-gonna tell you, and if you can catch me, that's all right; and if you can't, that's all right, too. But I'm gonna tell you."

He said, "If you run, I'm gonna beat hell out of you."

I said, "The cat got in the 'lasses, Dad, and I tried to wash it off."

He said, "You hell-fired devil, you!"

Well, I left the field a-running. He didn't whip me too bad, but he give me a pretty bad shaking-up.

Now, them 'lasses, there wasn't no hairs in there nor nothing. They was just as clean, but we couldn't bear the stomach of it, you know. We just couldn't bear it. And that was a true story.

Stanley Hicks, 1911 Watauga County

Jack and the Heifer Hide

Now, this is a Jack tale. It's about Jack and Tom and Will. It'll take a little while to tell it, but it won't take too long.

The old man had three sons named Jack and Tom and Will. And he told these boys, says, "Now, I've got some land out here, and I'll give it to you. If you'll go out there and clean it up, I'll give it to you. You can have it."

So he gave Tom a horse and Will a horse, and he give Jack a heifer. And they went out there, a-workin', a-workin', a-workin'. Jack was pretty lazy; he wouldn't do too much.

So they got kind of tired, you know. Tom and Will was having to do all the work. They said, "Jack, you go to the store" (old country store), "and get us some groceries, and we'll work while you're gone."

So they decided to cut a tree on his heifer and kill it. Thought that way they'd get rid of Jack. So while Jack was gone, his heifer was browsing around there, and they cut a big tree on it and killed it.

Jack come back, and they said, "Jack, we had awful bad luck, the worst luck in the world."

"You had?" he said. "What happened?"

Said, "Your heifer was browsing, and we didn't know it, and we cut a tree on it and killed it."

"Huh! Bydads! That's all right. That's all right."

So he went out there and he skinned this heifer out, dressed her out real good. Hung the hide up on the porch to dry. And he set around there and eat meat, steak, and all. He was just gettin' fat as could be.

Tom and Will was just workin' like crazy. And so he got the heifer all eat up. Jack was gettin' plumb fat, you know. "Now," they said, "when Jack eats that up, we'll have to do something else."

So Jack got it all eat up. He went out and took his old heifer hide down, and sewed it up, you know. Sewed the hide up where he skint it out. Stuffed it full of shucks, dried shucks.

And he got it by the tail, and he started down the road a-draggin' it. Draggin' this old hide down the road. Walkin' down the road a ways. Got tired, wanted some water, and stopped at a house and pecked at the door.

Out come a lady. She said, "What do you want? What are you doing here? What do you want, anyhow?"

He said, "Well, I want somewhere to stay all night. Want something to drink. Got tired."

She said, "We don't keep no strangers. You'll have to go on down the road." Jack, he went on down the road, draggin' this old hide.

Come to another house. He pecked on the door, and out come a woman with a broom in her hand. She looked at Jack, and she said, "What do you want, anyhow?" Said, "What are you doin' here?"

He said, "Well, I want a place to stay all night." Said, "I'm tired, wore out."

She said, "We don't keep no strangers. You'll have to go on down the road."

Well, Jack, he was gettin' wore out; it was gettin' plumb late, up agin about dark. He took this old hide and dragged it on down the road. Come on down, come to a big old two-story log house. Great, big old house.

He went up and banged on the door and out come a woman, not too big a woman. She looked at him and said, "What in the world do you want? What are you doing here?"

He said, "Well, I want a place to stay all night. I'm gettin' hungry and tired. Wore out."

She said, "Well, we usually don't keep no strangers. But you can go upstairs. You'll have to go upstairs."

He said, "Bydads! That's all right." So Jack drug this old hide, and he went on upstairs.

And this woman had another man, you know. Her man was workin' out, but she had another one, you know, a parson.

And so there was Jack upstairs, and there was a big hole in the log, and he was lookin' down through this hole. Watchin' her. She was a-bakin' bread, pie, stuff, puttin' 'em in the cupboard. Roasted a pig; roasted a turkey. Put it in the cupboard.

Jack just a-watchin', his mouth just a-waterin' just as hard as it could be.

Way up in the night, her husband come back and banged on the door. She said, "Huh? What are you comin' in here, wakin' me up this time of night, way up in the night, wakin' me up?"

She run and put this here parson down in the chest, locked him up! Jack was a-watchin' her.

Her husband said, "I been workin' late. Let me in!" So she run and let him in, and he said, "Honey, you got anything to eat?"

"Yeah," she said, "a little cold crust and mush over there." Jack was a-pullin' that old hide. "Clump. Clump."

Husband said, "What's that upstairs?"

She said, "Well, that's just a man come here a-draggin' a old hide.

Wanted to stay all night, and I told him he'd have to go upstairs to stay."

Jack comes down, and her old man says, "Hello, Stranger. What's your name?"

Jack says, "Jack." He comes draggin' this old hide down, come up beside the table.

The man said, "Have something to eat with me, Jack."

Jack took a bite or two of this old cold mush, and he just couldn't hack it atall.

So he knocked on the old hide, said to it, "Ah, shut up! There ain't nothing there."

Man said, "What did it say, Jack?"

"Ah, I couldn't tell you."

"Oh, come on, Jack."

"No, I couldn't tell you atall."

"Confound it, what did it say?"

"Well," said Jack, "it says there's some fruit bread and pie in the cupboard."

"Is it, old woman?" the man said.

"Yee-e-s," she said, "but I'm savin' it for my kinfolks, though."

Man says, "Well, me and Jack's kinfolks." So they got some of that and eat it.

Then Jack wanted to try that roasted pig and turkey. He bumped on it again. "Clump. Clump." On the old hide.

"Ah," he said, "shut up! Talk ain't goin' to get you nothin'."

"What did it say, Jack?"

"Oh," said Jack. "Couldn't tell it atall. It'd made the woman in the house mad."

"Oh, come on, Jack," said the man.

"No, it'd make her mad."

"What did it say?"

"Well, it said there was roasted pig and turkey down in the cupboard."

"Is there, old woman?" the husband said.

"Ye-e-e-s. Thought the kinfolks might like a little."

"Well, me and Jack's kinfolks." So they got out some of that meat there.

Old man said, "Jack, I've got to have that hide."

Jack said, "No, I couldn't sell it atall."

He said, "Yeah, I've got to have it. When I'm gone and come back, it'll tell me everything that's been going on."

"No," he said. "I couldn't sell it atall."

He said, "Yeah, I've got to have it. Come on, Jack, and sell me that hide."

"No, I couldn't."

"Jack, I've got to have it."

Said, "Well, I'll tell you what I'll do. I'll take that old chest and a thousand guineas." (You know, they called money "guineas" then.)

"No, you ain't a-gonna take my chest. My daddy give it to me; his daddy give it to him; his great-granddaddy give it to him! You ain't gonna take my chest off!"

"Yeah," said Jack. "I'll take the chest."

"No! My daddy give it to me; his daddy give it to him; his great-granddaddy give it to him; his great-uncle give it to him—*Oh! Confound the granddaddies!* Take the chest on!"

They traded.

And Jack, he watched it all night. You know, watched to see that the old parson didn't get out of that chest. So the next morning, the old man got up, and Jack said, "Now, you'll have to help me load this here chest."

So they got it out on the porch and scooted it off on Jack's back. Well, Jack just ba-r-e-ly could go with it. It was so heavy, you know, with that old parson in it. Just barely could get out of sight of the house. Got around the side of the house. Jack said, "Confound! Confound this old heavy chest! I'm just gonna throw it right down this well!"

"Pray don't, Jack!" Said, "The old parson's in here. If you don't throw it down the well, I'll poke you out a thousand guineas, out this here crack."

Jack said, "Poke 'em out right quick!" so he set the old chest down, and the old parson poked him out a thousand guineas.

Jack, he went on home and was tellin' Will and Tom about all the money he got out of his heifer hide. They said, "We don't believe it; you're lying."

He showed 'em the money. And they run out and took the old muzzle-loaders and shot the old horses down, skint 'em out, stuffed 'em full of shucks and took 'em down the road. The flies got after 'em, a-blowin', people a-shootin' at 'em, and them a-runnin'.

Finally, they had to take 'em off and bury 'em. Went back. Said, "Jack, we come back to kill you! You lied!"

"No, I didn't!"

"Yeah, you did! We come back to kill you."

"Well, Bydads! That's all right."

So they got a big old sack, and they got Jack in and took him down to a big old hole at the river and got a big rock to put in to drown him. Well, they got to studying. "Now, if we drown him, we won't be able to find his money. We'll go back and get the money before we drown him."

So while they was gone back, there come an old sheepherder along. Old man, had a thousand head of sheep and a nice horse. And Jack, a-kickin' around in that bag. He went up, said, "What are you doing in there, Stranger? What's your name, anyhow?"

He said, "Jack."

Old man said, "What are you doin' in there, anyhow?"

He said, "I'm fixin' to go to heaven."

Said, "Fixin' to go to heaven?"

"Yeah, fixin' to go to heaven. There's gonna be two angels come, a-talkin' along directly. They're gonna take me to heaven, and I'm fixin' to go!"

He said, "Jack, let me go. I'm gettin' old and all. Wore out."

"No," Jack says. "Bydads! I'll just go while I've got a opportunity to go."

"Come on and let me go."

"No, I couldn't do that atall. I might not get another chance."

Said, "Jack, let me go. I'll give you a thousand head of sheep and this nice horse."

"Well, Bydads! Untie the sack!"

So the old man untied the sack, and Jack got out and tied him up in there and said, "Now, listen! Before you get ready to go, there'll be two angels come a-talkin' along. Don't you speak to neither one. If you do, you won't get to go. They won't take you. They'll find out they've got the wrong man, and they won't take you." Well, Jack got the sheep back out in the woods, and he hid 'em and hid the horse.

Here come Tom and Will, a-talkin' along, you know, and they picked up the old sheepherder and pitched him over in the river. He kicked and kicked and finally went down. Jack waited till they got back to the house, and he got on this horse and got to shoutin', "Hey! Hi! Hey! Hi! Ho! Hup!"

Got on up to the house. And Tom said, "Lord, have mercy! That must be Jack! Can't be him! We drowned him, I know."

"Hey! Hi! Ho! Hup! Hey! Hi! Ho! Hup!"

"Lordy mercy!" Said, "That's Jack, all right!"

He come on up, and they said, "Jack, we thought we was a-drownin' you, and here you come with a thousand head of sheep and a nice horse. How in the world did you get 'em?"

He said, "Huh! Bydads! You thought you was drownin' me, but I was standin' up there with the sheep."

They said, "Jack, you broke us up every way on earth. Take us back and throw us in and let us get something."

Jack said, "No! Ain't gonna do it!"

"Please, Jack."

"No, ain't gonna do it."

"Come on, Jack."

"Well," he said, "help me build a little corral to put my sheep in, and I'll go back and put you boys in." So they did, and he said, "Get two good strong sacks."

So they got two strong sacks and went back. And Tom was heavier than Will, you know. So Jack said, "Now, you'll have to help me throw Tom in." So they put Tom in and give him a chug over in there, and he was kicking, drowning, going down, you know.

Will said, "What's he doing, Jack? What's he doing?"

"Oh," says Jack, "he's gettin' up his sheep." Says, "He's just about to get up a thousand head more."

"Oh," said Will, "put me in just as quick as you can. Tie me up and throw me in just as far as you can."

So Jack put him in there and tied him up and hove him off that big rock. He went down into the water and drowned.

Jack felt just awful, so he went back to the house. And the last time I seed Jack, he had the prettiest woman and was doing the wellest I've ever seed any man in my life!

And that was the last of that Jack story!

Stanley Hicks, 1911 Watauga County

Telling the Tales

Now, there ain't nobody that can tell them the same way every time. It's like I said while ago, about the preachers. If the word's a-comin' to you, if you tell it free from your mind, you're going to tell it by the words that come each time, and they don't come alike every time.

But now, if you're a-trainin' on it, you'd try to tell it exactly. But you couldn't. Keep practicing. That's why they like it everywhere I've been a-tellin' 'em, cause they say I tell 'em different.

Now, a lot of times you'll not get in everything. Now, that time, I'd say I got about all of it in the way I was taught.

Now, the Jack tales. Richard Chase come through this country when I was just a young boy, gettin' the tales. And he got some from my grandfather. But all the tales that he got from him I had heard when I was just a kid. From my grandfather down here. He knowed 'em all.

Now, I was down here when he was a-gettin' them from my grandfather. I remember. Now, "Jack and the Fire Dragon," my grandfather told me it.

Now, they was all translated in the book from the way they told 'em. The way they told 'em, they was too rough to put down! Gosh! They was rough! Rough words in 'em.

My grandfather told him some he couldn't hew down. They was so many bad words in it, he couldn't fix it to put it in the book.

Now, there was one where Jack went with another woman. But it's different now. He might could a-hewed it down now, the way they tell things anymore.

But I never did use any bad words. The way I'd tell 'em to the kids, they liked 'em. I never did say *dammit* nor *dern* nor *hell* nor anything like that. The others would start a-tellin' 'em, and out would roll a bad word afore they thought.

But I never did start tellin' 'em on up till after my grandfather passed away. Now, when we was little, that was our entertainment, to hear him tell Jack tales, ghost tales, or Indian tales.

Gosh, I can remember them Indian tales! And wild boar tales!

Now, I can remember a short Indian tale now. This man and woman was a-livin' in this log cabin. Just him and her. The young'uns was all married and gone.

And they had one milk cow, just one milk cow for the milk and butter. And they said the cow didn't come in for two or three days. Couldn't find it; husband couldn't find it nowhere.

But after about a week, the cow with that bell come off of the mountain. "Ding-dong. Ding-dong!" Come on down to the log cabin. Picked a little bit. Around, a-pickin'. Laid down.

Said his wife said, "My cow's come back. Give me the milk bucket so I can go milk."

But the husband said, "Hold it! They's something wrong. A cow don't do that, pick a little bit and lay down that quick." Said, "Let me have my rifle."

And he loaded up his hog rifle, cracked down on the cow, and out rolled a dead Indian. They'd skinned the cow out and saved the hide. Covered his legs and mounted the skin on hisself to steal the woman. Wanted to get his wife.

See, she would have gone out to milk.

Yeah, now, that tale is true! But then, they's some that would say they'd wish to the devil he had a-got their wife!

Ray Hicks, 1922 Watauga County

Chapter 10. Ghosts, Haints, and Witches

Everybody likes a good fright! The western Carolinian differs only in that he likes his scares to be more vivid, perhaps, and told with relishing detail. Ghost and haint tales are alive in many families; from time to time even now one encounters an old-timer who solemnly swears to a personal encounter.

Witch stories abound, still lingering from a day when neighbors were given to regarding each other's idiosyncrasies with awe and suspicion, seasoned with a lively imagination. Superstitions varied from one family to another, and the crops and gardens were sure to be planted by the "signs."

Telling the Difference

Now,
a haint,
you *see* it,
and a ghost,
you don't see it,
you *hear* it.
Now,
that's your difference.
You don't see a ghost,
but you'll see a haint.
And you'll hear a ghost.

Stanley Hicks, 1911 Watauga County

Where the Tales Came From

Now, these old tales was handed down from generation to generation. I've heard my grandma sing old songs and tell the ghost tales and the haint tales and the Jack tales.

See, there was a ghost tale, a haint tale, and a Jack tale. Now, these haint tales and these ghost tales, they's a lot of them that's true and a lot that ain't.

Now, this is where they got the foxfire at. Some of us calls it "spunk." I'm going to tell you the whole story. I'm a jack-of-all-trades; I can bring it to you, the whole works. People calls this "spunk," but it's foxfire. You see this hole in it? You see where I sawed it in two with the chain saw? See, this grows in hollow trees in a maple or a oak. No, it ain't mushroom; it's just really foxfire.

Well, I could take this out here and let it rain on it tonight. And you'd see it and think it was the devil. See, here's its nose, its eyes. It's a-glowing in the night — looks like fire. Has to get wet first.

Now, you can go to the woods and see all these haints and ghosts and stuff in these stumps a-lookin' at you, ready to jump on you. Well, here it is; this is it.

Well, I can take two rocks, flint rocks, get me off some of this, and catch a fire. That's what they built a fire with. You could catch it, you see, just like that. And that's the reason they called it foxfire.

Now, too, they'd build a fire with powder. Take 'em a little pile of rags, pour 'em out some powder — black gunpowder — in the fireplace, put rags over it. Then they'd take flint rocks, and the spark would catch it. And it would run up in there and catch the rags a-fire and start a fire. No, the gunpowder wouldn't blow up. They just put a little bit.

So my uncle, when he went to take it out of his horn, he poured it in here, and when he drug his horn back, he drug a streak back behind and left it a-laying with no stopper in it.

Well, it caught and run back here and caught the horn a-fire and near about blowed him out of the house. Didn't kill him, but about blowed him out of the house. Blowed the horn up. Busted the horn.

Stanley Hicks, 1911 Watauga County

The Back Bedroom

I was datin' a girl over here at Boone, North Carolina. Three kids, two boys and a girl was all they ever raised. Now, that board house that they had was hainted. Hainted in the back room, just like that back room in there!

I didn't know it, and I got down there that Saturday night and stayed with 'em and with the girl. When I started to leave [to walk home through the canyon], her pappy spoke up and said, "Hold it, Ray."

I said, "What's wrong?"

He says, "Hold it. I want you to sleep in that back room tonight."

I says, "Why?"

He says, "I thought you was lying to me. I thought you was staying with some of my neighbors up here. I thought no man—even a grown man—would have went home where you live, with no light nor nothin', through that dark canyon. But I asked them, and I know they're truthful. They said they hadn't seed you."

I said, "No, I'd a-went home. I wouldn't lie to nobody."

He said, "Well, I know a lot of boys would like to hold up brave, tell it that they went home when they didn't."

I said, "No, if I'd a-stayed with 'em, I'd a-told you."

"Well," he said, "that's why I asked them, and that's why I want you to stay in that room."

I says, "Why do you want me to stay in there?"

"Well," he said, "my wife's mother and sister come down here to stay all night in the middle of the week, and we put 'em in there to sleep and," said, "in a few minutes they was in there a-screamin', and I went in there and got 'em out. They said something got on to 'em, and the mother said she saw the awfullest face lookin' in at the window, aside of the old chimney."

Said, "I laughed at 'em and went in and told 'em, boy, they was people! Told 'em I was raised back in a canyon where they *was* ghosts." Said, "I was raised with ghosts, where they *was* ghosts, part of my life."

Said, "They ain't nothin' in there. And I went in there, and it run *me* out! It put *me* out! And I want to see if it'll put you out. I know you's brave after I asked them, and they said you've went home at night." Said, "You've got me beat. I wouldn't have went home arter I stay arter night. Specially not with no knife or gun. Don't believe I'd go with a gun arter night through there."

And then he said, "Will you stay?"

"Well, my mother's at home," I said. "And she never would close her eyes." That's why I'd try to get home. Mother never would close her eyes till she'd hear that door open. Two o'clock in the morning, or three, or whatever time I got in. She never did sleep a wink. Well, I'd try to get in about eleven o'clock or midnight, not no later than midnight.

He spoke, and he says, "Well, she won't die in one night." Said, "She'll make it, and you can go home in the morning, Sunday." That was on a Saturday night.

I said, "Well." And so, on up, we talked. They wasn't no lights in the country then. Just kerosene lamps with a chimney on 'em.

Directly, the girl took a kerosene lamp and went back there and fixed the bed and come back in there and smiled at me and said, "Ray, have a good night."

Well, I talked on about another thirty minutes and then went on in. Thought, well, if I do it and don't back out, I might as well just face the ghost. I'm a-goin' in!

I said, "Well, they's one thing I can tell you. You'll either find my dead body in that room, or I'll be there alive in the morning. But I won't leave."

He said, "You'll slip out and go home."

I says, "No, if it does throw me out, I won't leave; I'll come back in here."

You know, he knowed a lot of old tales and could sang old songs that's been forgot. Boy! I loved to hear that. I says, "I'll just wake you up, and we'll set by the fireplace, and you can tell me old tales and sang songs till daylight."

So I went on and got in bed, and she come and got the lamp. She looked at me again, and she says, "Ray, I love you. But I wouldn't sleep in here for a million dollars. They ain't *nothin'* that could get me to sleep in here. If anything runs my daddy out, it must be bad!"

I says, "Maybe your dad's got you fooled! Maybe he ain't afraid, but he's just got to thinking he is. You know, they's a lot that does that."

My dad was that way. He'd boast that he was brave till the rats got in Mother's chickens, and then I had to go out and get the rats out. And me young! I was just young, and Dad was huntin' for the ghost. Well, I just went on out and got the rats out. I killed two or three big wharf rats with my hands out there in the dark. They's arter them diddles, Mother's diddles, what was hatched out. That's the only way she had to get a little money when I growed up.

I says, "Well, I'm goin' to try it in the bed." And so she went out with the light, and I was a-layin' flat o' my back.

Directly, I was a-dozin' off, and the cover felt like it slipped down. My chest was chilly. It was in the fall of the year. Frost.

I felt in the dark, and the cover hadn't moved. Just felt that way!

And I laid a few more minutes, dozin', and the cover slipped again, felt like it. And I put my hand up and felt, and it hadn't moved. I said, "Eh, somethin' just a-makin' it feel that way!"

So I said, "Now, I'm gonna lock my hands! I'm gonna lock my hands in the dark and squeeze right tight and see how it feels." And when I done that, the bed picked up and floated. Felt just like it picked up and floated over just like my body was a-layin' in the bed across the hearth.

Well, I thumped my fist agin the wall. Says, "Well, I know spirits don't move beds!" Well, the bed wadn't moved. But my body felt just like it was on the hearth! See, now, it was dark as pitch in there!

And so I layed there about fifteen minutes, what you'd guess at, and the bed just shuddered! Felt like it floated back where it left from. And that ended it. I went to sleep, slept good.

Woke up the next morning and went in there. Went round by the porch, and the old man was settin' by the fire.

"All right, I'm here! I slept the night in the room," I says.

He says, "Tell us what happened."

I says, "She's just about got breakfast ready, your wife. I'll just wait. It's a long story."

So she got breakfast ready, and we eat. I got to talkin' about something else, and it kindly left my mind. So arter while, he said, "Ray, let's hear that."

I first pulled his leg. I says, "Well, they's enough wharf rats in there, that they tried to cut every bit of my hair off to build 'em a bed."

He said, "Now, Ray, I know wharf rats. Now, what did it do?"

I said, "Well, the cover slipped down . . . "

He said, "Now, that's when I got out of there! Let's hear the rest."

See, he'd got out when it one time slipped. He said, "Now, what happened when it slipped the first time?"

"Well, it slipped agin. Felt like it. Then I put my hands on the cover arter the second time, and then it floated the bed."

Well, it went on, and another feller bought the place. So I was tellin' him about that room in there, and he didn't believe in nothin' like that. He said, "Ray, it ain't no haints. Dead people don't come back." He said, "When anything's dead, it's dead. Right over yonder is a branch you cross, over yonder. They all seed a woman over there with a white dress on, and her hell-fired head cut off."

Oh, he was gettin' old. Ill talkin'. He said, "Well, I went through there. Got through that branch. Went down there, and there was that hell-fired woman with her white dress on and her hell-fired head cut off.

"Well, I hunted in the hell-fired branch for three hell-fired rocks."
(That was his by-word, hell-fired.)

Said, "I throwed the hell-fired first one. Missed her." Said, "I throwed
the hell-fired second one. Missed her." Said, "It was dark there at night
and me with no light. Well, the third one hit her, and Pup-Pupp! Pup-
Pupp! Pup-Pupp!"

Well, I went back over there the next morning, and I'd killed one of
my brother's geese! So I went down to my brother and said, 'Here, let
me pay you. I killed that woman up yonder last night.'"

So he said, "Now, that's the way it is with yourn in that room. It ain't
nothin' in there."

So it went on, him a-stayin' in that house, and him a-gettin' old. And I
was down there on Saturday to see his son. His mother said he'd gone to
Boone.

I said, "Well, I'll just go on in and see the old man." I loved him. I
always liked to hear him talk. Plain talking.

Well, I went on in and talked to him a while. Him a-gettin' feeble.
Nearly dead. So I started to leave, and there was a old footlog over a
branch and a old log barn yet up there. I got on that footlog to leave and
seed him a-comin' with his cane a-wavin', nearly fallin'.

And I said, "Wonder if he's a-wantin' to speak to me afore I leave." I
just waited, and he come up by the path.

I said, "Are you a-wantin' to tell me somethin?"

He said, "Yeah, Ray. You knowed what you was a-talkin' about. They
was somethin' in that room." Said, "The one that built that house, his
wife told that he'd hid fifteen hundred dollars somewhere. She thought
he'd hid it under a apple tree, and everyone that had rented it had
grubbed the apple trees, and they wasn't but three left of the old apple
trees.

"And the old feller's wife had told that he went out of that room with
a fruit jar, and she figgered he hid the fifteen hundred dollars under one
of them apple trees."

But he said, "Ray, I went to remodel that room and took the old
hearth up, and in there was the old cement where the old jar was at!"

Now, that's why the bed went on the hearth! The money was in it!
And if I'd just a-spoke and said, "Oh, Lord, what are you appeared to me
for?" it would have said, "It's fifteen hundred dollars under the hearth
here."

And that old man that I had stayed with had built a new house. He
said he owed nobody nothin'. I knowed he had no money, and fifteen

hundred dollars back yonder would of built three houses! Them old box houses.

It could have been God put it in me to let them have it! They had three children and was a-havin' it rough.

Ray Hicks, 1922 Watauga County

A Confederate Ghost

Lieutenant William Penland
was a Confederate soldier
eighteen years old,
stationed in Tennessee.
And one day his sweetheart
saw him coming,
riding horseback.
She went into the house a minute
to fix her hair.
And when she came back out,
he had disappeared.
His mother, also,
saw the same thing.
That was the day he died in service.

Thelma Penland Axley, 1906 Cherokee County

The Hitchhiker

One time
there was a man coming up the road,
and he said
that something got on behind him.
On a horse.
His daughters had told him
that house down there was haunted.
So he was a-ridin' along,
and he was about half drunk.

And something,
he said,
just like some person,
just got behind him and held to his sides.
And when he come to the next branch,
it got off.

I guess that sobered him!

Tennie Cloer, 1886 Cherokee County

The Disappearance

Here's a story we was told all the time we was growing up. About this woman. She left her husband. He was sick, had heart dropsy. He was-settin' by the fire in a rocking chair when she left the house, and she went out to the edge of the woods to get an armful of wood.

She threw it over the fence, and said, about that time here he come, walking up there. And he went up. Just disappeared. That was my husband's uncle and his wife.

She saw him go up in the air—go on up. Said he had on the same clothes that he had when he was settin' by the fire. See, she had just left the house, and he was settin' there by the fire.

So, when she got back in the house then, he was dead. And she had seen him go past. She's a truthful woman. A Christian woman.

Ruth Sturgill, 1893 Alleghany County

An Invitation

One day this man was passing Little Pine Church. He had been to see his girlfriend. He was dating this girl. And they said he was passing the cemetery there at Little Pine Church, and he hollered, "Come on, Ezerette."

Ezerette Bowman was buried there, and he hollered, "Come on, Ezerette."

He was on a horse, you know, riding horseback. And there come something. He seen something just rise up out of the cemetery and just get on the horse behind him!

And he run his horse home! It was about a mile from where Preacher Handy lived. He was Preacher Handy's son. He just run his horse home. And they said he just fell in the door!

Mrs. Handy had to go put the horse up. And when he went to see that girl anymore, he'd go around the other way.

Why, he didn't know what it was! He just saw something come up out of the cemetery. You know, he was hollering to the dead there, "Come on." And it come.

Rosa E. Carpenter, 1893 Alleghany County

The Appearance in the Cemetery

When I was a little girl on the farm, we had a hired hand by the name of Mr. Lee Summerlin. He was a very colorful character. I very well remember the dog that was always with him. That was Old Blue.

And Old Blue would go out and tree possums in the night. Mr. Summerlin might wake up and hear him barking and go in the dead of the night to get the dog to hush barking and get the possum.

But he came to our house every day that was a work day. If my father had things for him to do, he would feed the horse and take real good care of everything. We all learned to love Mr. Summerlin very much.

One thing he used to tell us was this story that he insisted was the real truth! And he is said to have been—and he would tell us, himself— a rather "wild young fellow." He was an only son. He had one sister.

And when he was young, he wanted to do as *he* wanted to do, and he liked to drink a little whiskey along with it. He would describe his pearl-handled pistol to us. And he would tell us that he always carried that for "safety's sake."

So one time in the fall, everyone was gathering in the corn and piling it in great piles by the crib where it would be shucked and thrown into the crib for keeping for the winter. And so different people would invite you to their corn shuckings.

Usually people would come along in the afternoons, and they would have a big supper cooked for everyone. But this one was to be at night, and he told his mother that he had been invited to the corn shucking.

And she said, "Now, Lee, you are not to go to that corn shucking because there will be a rowdy crowd of boys there, and you'll get into real trouble."

"Now, Ma, I am determined that I am going to that corn shucking." So she talked to him each day about not going, and he talked about the fact that he *was* going.

So, finally, he announced to her, "Now, Mother, I'm going to this corn shucking, no matter what anybody says!"

She says, "Yes, and I do hope that as you pass by that cemetery, that something just rises right up and gets you!"

And he said, "Knowing my mother, she'd easily get somebody to go up there and scare me."

In those days, places like church houses or gardens or fields of crops were fenced in because it was in the days of free range, and nobody put up their cattle or hogs or sheep or anything. They just roved wherever they chose. And all the things that were to be taken care of were fenced in.

So, to find the church, you had to go through two different gates, because there was an enclosure around the entire cemetery and church.

So, he said that on the evening that he was going to the corn shucking, he dressed and saddled his beautiful little bay mare that he rode. And he was that dashing young man that the ladies liked.

He put his pistol, he said, in his pocket where it would be very easily gotten to. And he meant to use it if anybody at that church cemetery tried to scare him.

So he went on to the corn shucking, and everything turned out as they had planned. Lots of fun, because if you found a red ear of corn in the shucking, you got to kiss your favorite girl.

And, many times, there was a jug of whiskey hidden in the center of the pile of corn. Now, whether there was one on this particular night, I don't know, but he had promised his mother faithfully that he would not drink that night.

And he would always say to us, "And I lived up to my promise. I did not take a drink of whiskey that night."

But, anyway, as the corn was finished around eleven or twelve o'clock, he said he started on his way home. And the moon had risen over the mountain and was just beautifully bright. "And," he said, "you didn't have any trouble finding your way at all because it was just almost as bright as day."

So he traveled along and got to the gate at the end of the enclosure that he'd have to open to go through by the cemetery. The road ran right in front of the cemetery and the church. He said he thought to himself, "No use to be scared because it's so bright I can see everything."

And, as he got back up on his horse after closing the gate, he noticed something rising right out about the center of the cemetery.

"And," he said, "I just immediately drew out my pistol because I knew Ma" (as he called her) "had gotten somebody to come and scare me."

"So," he said, "I got that little pistol ready, and I thought, now if they come one step toward me, I'll really use this to scare them half to death!"

But as the figure started moving, it just lighted up. And it was adult sized. "And," he said, "it was the most beautiful angel that you could ever imagine. It was prettier than anything I have ever seen in a picture book."

"And," he said, "if I thought the moon was bright, the light around the angel was so much brighter that you just couldn't even imagine it."

As she came tripping across; her feet seemed to barely touch the ground, and she came right straight over to the road where he was and walked right along beside him. "And," he said, "the horse just didn't seem to pay any attention."

He said, "I wasn't exactly frightened. It was just a feeling of awe I had. Of course," he said, "I dropped my pistol long before this time, and she just walked right on down beside me as I rode my horse till I got to the other end of the fence around the cemetery and the church. Then I had to get off to open the gate. And when I did, the light was gone. And when I turned around, she was gone."

And he said, "This made me think, now, this is not my imagination. I know it couldn't be because God just sent this to prove to me that I couldn't disobey my mother without him a-knowin' it."

Of course, when I knew Mr. Summerlin, he was just a great character, always just so fine. And yet, I had heard him tell that he once had liked to take a drink and be rowdy and that this is what worried his mother.

My grandfather told us that he had known Lee Summerlin, and other older people in the community had known him also. And they said that was a turning point in his life, that he had changed at that point and had never gone out in the community and been rowdy anymore.

Marie McNeil Hendrix, 1913 Wilkes County

The Bonepicker

Now I'll tell you a ghost tale. Now, just like these tales is, part of it is true. And part of it is lies and black lies and bare-faced lies. But part of this is really true.

There was an old man, now, and he worked off of his sawmill. He was drunk all the time, and he treated his family awful cruel. See, they told me this now, my grandpa and them. I didn't see this, but they told it to me.

And he'd come in every weekend a-drinkin', a-cussin', a-screamin', and a-hollerin' at night, you know, abusing his family, treating 'em awful bad, they said. Well, one night they heard him hollerin' and cussin', and they thought he was just drunk.

And back at that time, now—they tell this for the fact; I don't know, but they'd tell it back in the old days—they said that there was a thing that when it killed you, it would take all the meat off of your bones. Called it a "bonepicker." It was a animal back in the old days. I don't know what it was, but my grandpa said it would eat all the meat off the bones and just leave the bones.

So it had eat all his meat off of his bones. It was all gone the next morning when they found him. And they buried him very close by the house, my grandpa said.

And at night, at that time, every weekend at night they could hear him a-hollerin', you know, hollerin' and takin' on and screamin'.

And they could hear these things. Now, that was probably imagination. I don't know. I always thought it was. But they could hear these things: "We're gonna pick your bones! We're gonna pick your bones!" [a shrill cry]

And they would get closer to the house, closer to the house. Well, that family, they pulled out and left.

See, the old people, they didn't know whether it was really a spirit or something doing this or whether it was their imagination.

So, in the neighborhood there was an old man, a real old fellow. And he said, "I'll go, and I'll find out what it is." And they told this for the truth. I don't know. I can't say, but some of it probably is true. And so this old man, he went there at the time this thing would come, and this man would holler and scream and make this racket.

You'd never see it, but you'd hear it. But a haint, you can see it.

So he went, and he fixed the door good. Had a big old chimney to it, he said. Fixed the door and fixed the windows; it had two or three windows. Anyway, he fixed it so nothing couldn't get in. And he went in the house.

So, along in the night, everything got real still and quiet, they said. So after while he heard this thing a-coming. "I'm gonna pick your bones! I'm gonna get you!"

He heard, "Stomp! Stomp! Stomp!" Getting closer. And that old man, he was a-settin' in this house. And it come up to the window. It would say, "I'm gonna pick your bones!" But it couldn't get in.

So it went on around to the door. "I'm gonna pick your bones. I'm gonna get you!" Came around, but it couldn't get in at the door.

Well, it goes on around to another window. "I'm gonna pick your bones. I'm a-comin' in."

And he just set there. Scared, probably, to death! After a while, everything got still. But he had forgot about the chimney. Then he heard it clump on the floor! Come down the chimney and hit the floor.

"I done got you. Now, I'm gonna pick your bones!"

Well, he just takes the hinges off of the door! He just takes it all out, and away he goes! He runs just as hard as he can go.

And he comes to a muddy place. He runs into this mud and all, and his tongue's hung out. So he just gives up and falls over. Just lays there with his tongue hanging out on the ground. That's the way my grandpa used to tell it.

Well, he lays there till he thinks this thing's gone. But after while he hears, "Clump! Clump! Clump! I'm gonna pick your bones. I'll get you!"

He tries to raise up. Tries to raise up, but he can't get up. You know, he's just almost gone. And it's a-gettin' closer all the time.

"I'm gonna get you. I'm gonna pick your bones!"

And that time he comes up! He runs just as hard as he can go, and he comes to a big bridge where a big creek is at. Well, he comes to this big footlog. He is scared so bad, he don't try to cross the bridge or footlog! He just runs through the water!

Well, a haint or ghost won't go through the water. You go through the water, and they won't follow you another foot. So he runs over to the other side, and he falls down. That's the way they tell it to me, now. He falls down on the ground and lays there — "Whew! Pant! Puff! Whew!"

"I'm gone this time, I know," he says to hisself. And then he hears it come to the creek.

"I'm gonna get you." Then everything hushes. And he lays there till near about daylight and then gets up and goes on back home. He gets in the bed along about daylight. Wet. Nasty. He's just chilled.

And his wife says, "What happened?"

He don't tell her. He just goes to bed.

Well, the neighbors, they come in. They said, "Now, Granviile, what did you see last night? What did you hear and what did you see out there? We just come to find out. Hey! Get him out of the bed. Get him a cup of coffee!"

So he gets out and sets in a chair, but he is so nervous. And they keep asking him what he heard and what he saw.

He said, "I'll tell you. I never seed a dag-gummed thing! And I never heard a dag-gummed thing! And if you're gonna find anything out, you're gonna have to go out there yourself."

Now, part of that is really true. That was really true about the voice. And that old mean man, most of him was eat up. His head wasn't gone, but all of his arms and all of his legs and everything. No, it wasn't panthers. They called it a bonepicker.

Stanley Hicks, 1911 Watauga County

The Holy Ghost Dove

Now, what they call the Holy Ghost Dove, from God, was when somebody was going to get killed or pass away like my grandfather was, up here, my mother's dad.

And nobody knows why, but some people will bring 'em, just one now and then, from God. And, you know, I could bring one when I'm going away. Just three days afore I die, there could come a dove. I could bring one.

It's the way some people sees. The way they live. Now, this is true. This is a true tale.

Now, it's the Spirit of God descending in a dove shape. A white dove, whiter than anything you've ever seed on earth. And it comes three days before that person's breath leaves 'em. They'll go quicker than that, but they won't live no longer than that.

I've just seed two in my life. Seed two. And, boys, they's something to look at! And it makes you think of God when you see one of them. I've seed two in my life.

And so Mother's dad, up there, my grandfather, he was dying. I was a-runnin' an old '33 model Chevrolet truck I'd worked and got. Kept it a-runnin'. Put a '46 motor in it. And Mother said, "Ray, would you run me up to my dad's? They've sent after me. Say he's near about gone."

Well, I run her up there, and we's settin' there. And the way the house was built was in this L style. The chimney was this old homemade brick. Big hearth. We was settin' right at the end of it.

Had two windows. Ten to twelve old window lights in 'em. And so Grandmother was talkin' to Mother, speakin', and him a-layin' over there in the bed. And she said, "He's a-leavin'."

About that time, something struck that left window, comin' out of the east — now, they come out of the east — gone about ten or fifteen minutes and come back out of the west.

She said, "What was that, Renie?" Her oldest daughter was Renie.

Said, "I'll tell you sometime."

But I seed a glimpse of it. White. Just struck the window and went on. She said, "What broke that glass?" It had broke every bit of the glass out.

Her daughter said, "Mama, I'll tell you sometime." And she went over to pick the glass up.

And they was a-talkin' about fifteen or twenty minutes later, and it come back, and I seed it go by pretty good that time. White. Hit the other window on the other side of the chimney. She said, "There it is again! What is that?"

Her daughter said, "I'll tell you sometime."

When she went to leave, she said, "Mom, now I know. I've seed 'em before. Now, Dad'll be dead in no longer than three days."

And the third evening, he died.

Up here, then, the second one I seed, I was a-runnin' a '49 Chevrolet coupe then. And these here two buddies that I'd went herb gathering with had come up that night to see me. And we's just settin' up there talkin'.

And I was settin' under the steerin' wheel, and the older one was a-settin' next to me, and the younger one was settin' over on the other side, next to the door.

Well, we was a-settin', and I had a piece of old tarpaulin laid over my windshield to keep the sun from drawing the windshield out. Had no shed to put it in. Two rock laid on it.

Well, we set there and talked about ten or fifteen minutes, right up there to them rock piles. Here come the prettiest white thing you ever seed. Glowed up. I seed it afore they did.

And it just come toward the truck just like lightning. And they said, "What was that?" They argued that it was the wind. Said it moved them rocks. I got out. So, we was all just stifled there for a long time before we spoke. Sat.

I said, "What's wrong?"

They said, "Ray, that put a funny feeling on us."

I said, "Well, I'll tell you, right in the flesh, I'm a-feelin' weak."

They said, "Weak?"

I said, "Yes, 'cause one of us, or some of our people, is gonna be dead in three days. No longer than three days. I guess it's one of us. That was a Holy Ghost Dove."

They said, "A Holy Ghost Dove?"

I said, "Yeah." So that older one's dad was in the hospital. Operated on, and was fixin' to come home. And he hadn't went to see his dad nary time since he'd been in the hospital.

And his dad fell dead the third day.

Ray Hicks, 1922 Watauga County

The Ghost in the Chimney

And I'll tell you about a ghost, now. And we found out what it was. Now, they could hear this ghost, you know. It'd go sort of like chains a-rattling. It was in an old house and people wouldn't stay in it.

I was just small. I didn't care. Heck! And Dad, he didn't care for nothing. He said to me, "Let's go and see what that thing is."

And we went, and you couldn't hear it till way up in the night—ten o'clock. Chains would rattle; buckets would jingle. Yeah, we heard it.

It would go all the way around through the house. You would hear chains a-rattling down here and hear things in yonder. You'd go here and yonder.

And then Dad said, "Now, Stanley, you go down to the chimney." Had a chimney. It was an old log house. Two story. He said, "You go down to the chimney and listen, and I'll go up to the loft. And when it comes down there, you listen and see where it's at."

I said, "Well."

And so I went down there. Pretty scary in the dark; we didn't have no lights or nothing. So I went down there. And I heard, "Clunk—clunk—clunk. Clink—clink—clink. Jeeble—jeeble—jeeble." Awfullest racket.

And I said, "Daddy, here it is."

And he said, "It's back here."

And when we found it, you know what it was? It was a rat carrying black walnuts and dropping 'em down the chimney. The young'uns had dropped cans and stuff down in there, and the rat would drop the walnuts, and they would rattle. And it made so much racket that the people had left the house and wouldn't stay in it. Just on account of a rat.

Stanley Hicks, 1911 Watauga County

The Stone Mountain Witch

I was about seventeen years old, and my mother would tell me that by the Bible, now, there wadn't really no witch; said they ain't nothin' like that. Had me a-believin' they wadn't no witches. Well, now I know better! 'Cause I met up with one! I met up with a witch on that Stone Mountain yonder.

Dad was here, and us young'uns didn't have much to eat. Mother said, "The last bread flour is gone. You better take Ray and go to Stone Mountain and pull some evergreen galax."

Well, she fixed up a few cold biscuits, and we's a-gonna camp one night. There was another boy down here I growed up with, and he was a-goin' along to pull him some.

And Dad had bought a dog off a feller down yonder, and he was half bulldog. Would eat anybody up. He was one of them bad ones.

So we got on over there and had to walk on up that Pick-Breeches road. So we walked, it seemed like, about three miles up that mountain. And we got on up there and passed an old barn on the way, a-rottin' down. A log barn.

Well, we got on the other side of the mountain, on the Tennessee side, and my dad said he'd been in there when he was young, with his dad a-pullin' evergreens. He said, "It's growed up, kindly, but right here was the spring when I was a boy. We'll make our camp right here."

And he put me to see to the dog, and I tied it there with a chain. So then we pulled slabs off of a tree, where lightning had blowed 'em off, and made up a table and built one for a seat. Built us a fire. Put Irish potatoes in the fire to roast.

And about the time them 'taters was gettin' half done, it was gettin' dusty dark. I heard a racket going, "Will that dog bite? Will that dog bite?" Dog was just a-barkin'!

And I looked up, and there was a woman about sixty years old, I would say. Her hair was black as jet, hanging down, and her dress was in strings. And her feet was sticking out of her slippers where the soles had wore out.

I run up, and I said, "Oh, gosh, don't come by that dog!" I said, "He'll eat you up! Who are you anyhow?"

She just come on down, said, "Poor puppy." It just turned around and rolled up, just like it might of died. She said, "That dog won't hurt nobody now for about fifteen or twenty minutes. It'll not wake up for about that long." She said, "I'm not afraid of no dog nor no kind of animals. I just put 'em to sleep."

She had just waved her hand over it and said, "Poor puppy," and it just rolled over and went to sleep. It had just wagged its tail a little bit.

I said, "My gosh, did you kill my dog? You didn't kill my dog, did you?"

She said, "No, I just put it to sleep so it can't hurt nobody." And she said, "I just showed you my power. Just wanted to show you my power."

And so she went on down with me to the fire and welcomed herself to Dad and the other boy, a-settin' there. Said, "I'm hungry. Ain't had nothing to eat for three days but three raw onions. Would you give me something to eat?"

Dad told her, "Yeah." Said, "Wait till they get done." And in ten or fifteen minutes, he ruck her out a 'tater. Give her some salt. She eat.

Directly, she noticed, turned around, said, "Look up yonder, Son. See, I told you. Your dog's woke up." And it was doin' just like it was wakin' up. Got up. Wagged its tail. Droused around.

She said, "Your dog's all right." Said, "And I put just a little on you. You'll need it in your lifetime. I put just a little spell on you."

I reckon that's why I've been like I have, tellin' tales, I guess.

She said, "You'll be afeared of nothin' or nobody from now on. You can talk to the president or anybody. You won't be afeared to talk to nobody." Well, I hadn't from that day till now. She said, "I've fixed you for a good life."

And so she set there and eat. Then she asked Dad if she could use his pocketknife arter we went to bed. We had our cover fixed out there in the woods.

And we laid there. And Dad kept punchin' me, and he said, "Ray, they said they ain't no witches; but, gosh, I've lived to see a witch! You can't tell me that that woman settin' right there with my pocketknife ain't no witch."

He said, "I can't sleep. She'll slip over here and cut our throats with my pocketknife." We'd left her by the fire.

Well, I'd stuck my matches under the bark of an old dead chestnut. So it come a rain that night during the night, and our quilt between us had about a foot of water drippin' through on us when we woke up. So Dad hollered and said, "Get up there, Ray, and see if you can get a fire kindled up."

I got out there, and it was foggy and dark as pitch. I had to feel with my hands, a-huntin' for the camp-place and a-knowin' that witch was a-settin' there. Thinkin' she was. And I hunted the tree by feelin' and found my matches.

Rubbed one through my hair good so I could strike it on my overall buckle—now, you can take a match when it's damp and rub it through your hair and get that dampness off it, and it'll strike. Now, your hair has to be dry. See, my hair was under cover, and it hadn't got wet down in deep to the skull. Now, it was damp on the outside, but I rubbed the match down deep, next to the skull.

Well, I was a-doubtin' it, but it struck, and I took some of that bark of the tree out, some of that bark in next to the tree that burns so quick, got it out and lit it.

And when I got a light, that woman was gone! How in the world did she get out of there that dark a night? Foggy. She went up there and stayed in that old barn where she had been stayin'. She'd been stayin' in that barn and pullin' galax up in there. Makin' her a little money.

Ray Hicks, 1922 Watauga County

The Witch Doctor

Had witch doctors back then. My uncle made a witch doctor. He told me after then, said, "Harvey, that's tedious work, but you're young. If you want to, I'll learn you a lot about it." You know, I slipped around and told my mother.

And she said, "Harvey, don't you get into that. You'd have to be nothing, in a way. Not believe in the Lord." Said, "Don't you get in it. It'd ruin your life."

Now, this uncle, it was my daddy's brother. And their daddy had a heifer that got down, couldn't get up, just laid there. My uncle kept telling him, said, "Daddy, let me doctor that there heifer."

His daddy would say, "Ah, you can't do nothing for her. She's gonna die."

My uncle said, "If you'll let me, I'll guarantee she'll get up."

So one day my daddy was there and seen it. They'd all gathered there the day he was to do that. And he was a young man, you know. Said he walked out there, said, went all around that heifer. They thought she was dead, just laying there like she was dead. They couldn't get her to move.

And he walked all around it and put his hands on it. And they had a fire built. He cut a piece off its ear and said something, you know, some words. Said he walked off. Said it was gonna be better.

Told 'em all to watch. Said in an hour or two that heifer come up out of there bawling and took off to the hills.

Now, my uncle could stop blood. One time I had a tooth pulled. I was a-bleeding to death, and my brother went after him. My uncle lived over on the mountain. He come, and I was setting in a chair.

He went around me, saying words. And, in just a few minutes, my tooth stopped bleeding. You know, he was a doctor, doctored people. Yeah. Everybody liked him.

But he never did charge nothing.

And he'd tell fortunes. Girls' fortunes. He'd come there at home after he got old. Young folks would come in there and have the awfullest time a-laughing. He'd tell fortunes, you know. Then them young folks would give him a little money.

He'd tell by coffee grinds. You know, after the coffee is poured out. Turn that and he'd read that. And he'd read the palms of their hands. Now, my sister, before she died, she told me, "Harvey, I don't know whether you can remember it or not, but our uncle, Monroe Miller, he told me . . . ," said it happened what he had said.

He had told her, said, "You'll make a big trip. You'll go to the West to a man, but you'll never marry him."

And, years after that, she made that trip to Oregon. Stayed there, but her and that man never did marry. She told me, said that happened years after our uncle told her that.

No, he wouldn't tell you how he could do it. He'd look you right in the face and tell you things. He could tell by your expression some way. Yeah, he could tell you the past and the future.

He never did tell my fortune. It was girls, mainly, that he told. And their boyfriends.

Every night. They'd make a big pot of coffee and drink that coffee and tell fortunes. See, that was the way they spent time.

People have come from a long way off to get their fortunes told. You know, he moved to Erwin. Then, he told me he made a lot of money there in Erwin. There was another old woman there, but they'd come to him and say, "Monroe, we'd rather have you tell our fortunes than that old woman." Said, "You tell it more like it is."

He'd tell the bad and the good. Sometimes, I think, the girls would worry about it. He'd tell them they were going to lose their best boyfriends. They'd think, "What on earth will happen?" And they'd worry.

Now, my sister, she never would tell me all he told her. But she'd say, "I'm worried. Uncle Monroe told me. . . . " Said, "If that was to happen. . . . " Said, "I'm afraid I'm losing my best boyfriend."

Well, she did!

Harvey J. Miller, 1909 Mitchell County

The Turkey Witch

You know, there was some hunters that was bothered to death with an old turkey hen. They was hunting, and this old turkey hen bothered them to death, and they couldn't hunt.

It would get right around and jump, get right around and scratch. Make a noise. And they'd shoot at that old turkey and couldn't hit it. Bothered to death.

One man who heard of it said to get a silver bullet to shoot it. See, they'd found out it was a haint or witch, something like that. So he fixed him a bullet and got his old hog rifle and went out one morning, and he shot it.

Said when he shot it, that old turkey hen threw up and hollered and was gone! And he come on by. Said he thought he knew who it was. And sure enough, there was an old woman, and for a day or two she was in the bed, couldn't get up.

See, she was a witch. And he shot her with that silver bullet. She was in the form of that turkey hen. Yeah, she was in the bed, too. I remember her. My mother talked about her a whole lot. Said, "That's the old witch woman." She was a midwife.

Oh, she got over it and lived a long time, but she always limped after then. But they never was bothered with the turkey witch no more.

I remember where she lived. Back in the hollow. Everybody let her alone. She'd put spells on people, and didn't nobody want to get her mad. Wanted to stay in good standing with her.

One time a man had the best cow, giving a lot of milk, and she got mad at this man, and that cow went stone dry! Didn't give a bit of milk! Said that was where that old witch woman put a spell on it.

Harvey J. Miller, 1909 Mitchell County

Boogers

I never seen or heard anything in my life
that I wasn't satisfied what it was
before I left it.

One time there was a light
down yonder at the spring.
Said, "Let's go down there."
Couldn't get my brother to go.
Finally, made him go with me.
There was a powerful light down there,
right down there in the ground,
you know.

Went down there and the water had backed up
in the spring,
you know.
Moon shining right down in it.

The biggest boogers people see
would be like that
if they'd just go and see.

Tom Pruitt, 1904 Alleghany County